UNDERSTANDING

THE AMERICAN PAST

A Study Guide with Critical Thinking Exercises

Volume I: To 1877 • Fourth Edition

Richard L. Mumford

Elizabethtown College

Joseph R. Conlin

California State University, Chico

 THE HARCOURT PRESS

Harcourt Brace College Publishers

Fort Worth   Philadelphia   San Diego   New York   Orlando   Austin   San Antonio
Toronto   Montreal   Sydney   Tokyo

ISBN: 0-15-500616-9

Address Editorial Correspondence To: Harcourt Brace Jovanovich, Inc.
                                         301 Commerce Street, Suite 3700
                                         Fort Worth, Texas 76102

Address Orders To: Harcourt Brace Jovanovich, Inc.
                       6277 Sea Harbor Drive
                       Orlando, Florida 32887
                       1-800-782-4479, or 1-800-433-0001 (in Florida)

Printed in the United States of America

4 5 6 7 8 9 0 1 2   066   9 8 7 6 5 4 3 2

Contents

To the Instructor / v

To the Student / vii

1 A Collision of Worlds
America and Europe 25,000 B.C (?)–
A.D. 1550 / 1

2 England Goes to America
The Struggle to Plant a Colony,
1550–1624 / 11

3 Puritans and Proprietors
The Growth of Colonial America,
1620–1732 / 20

4 Colonial Society
English Legacies and Laws, American Facts of
Life / 27

5 The Other Americans
The Indians, French, and Africans of Colonial
North America / 34

6 British America in Bloom
The Colonies in the Eighteenth Century / 42

7 Years of Tumult
The Quarrel with the Mother Country,
1763–1770 / 49

8 From Riot to Rebellion
The Road to Independence, 1770–1776 / 57

9 The War for Independence
Winning the Revolution 1776–1781 / 66

10 Inventing a Country
American Constitutions, 1781–1789 / 74

11 We the People
Putting the Constitution to Work,
1789–1800 / 82

12 The Age of Thomas Jefferson
Expansion at Home, Frustration Abroad,
1800–1815 / 91

13 Beyond the Appalachian Ridge
The West in the Early Nineteenth
Century / 99

14 A Nation Awakening
Political, Diplomatic, and Economic
Developments, 1815–1824 / 107

15 Hero of the People
Andrew Jackson and a New Era,
1824–1830 / 114

16 In the Shadow of Andrew Jackson
Personalities and Politics,
1830–1842 / 123

17 A Culture in Ferment
Sects, Utopias, and Visionaries / 131

18 Heyday of Reform
Fighting Evil, Battling Social Problems / 138

19 A Different Country
The Evolution of the South / 147

20 The Peculiar Institution
Slavery as It Was Perceived and
as It Was / 155

21 From Sea to Shining Sea
American Expansion, 1820–1848 / 163

22 Apples of Discord
The Poison Fruits of Victory,
1844–1854 / 172

23 The Collapse of the Old Union
The Road to Secession,
1854–1861 / 181

24 Tidy Plans, Ugly Realities
The Civil War Through 1862 / 190

25 Driving Old Dixie Down
General Grant's War of Attrition,
1863–1865 / 200

26 Bringing the South Back In
The Reconstruction of the Union / 208

To the
Instructor

This Study Guide and the textbook it supports, Joseph R. Conlin's *The American Past*, Fourth Edition, bring together the two active functions of the historian—the narration and description of what happened in the past and the evaluation and analysis of why it happened and what it means.

In the teaching of history, two extremes emerge in the debate over whether an emphasis on descriptive subject matter or an emphasis on analytical thinking skills is best. One maintains that students must accumulate a large amount of data *before* they employ the historian's thinking skills. The assumption often is that students will recognize the thinking practices of the textbook author or of the professor from classroom lectures. The other insists that students must learn how to think *before* approaching data and ideas. The truth is that the accumulation of data and the development of thinking skills best occur *at the same time*—that is, the two must correlate and interact. They should not be separated. Data and ideas are acquired through a critical thinking process that can only be developed through an immersion in data and ideas.

Many books describe historical thinking. The uniqueness of this Study Guide is that it is made up of *exercises* to promote historical thinking, exercises in which the student can actually *practice* these thinking skills. The Study Guide follows the narrative text chapter by chapter and the most important skills exercises receive the most attention and are repeated for reinforcement in nearly every chapter. Students can do the exercises without the instructor's help. This practice will aid students in reviewing information and ideas and provide them with a self-evaluation of reading comprehension as well as gradually developing their critical thinking skills.

However, the best use of the guidebook would involve both the instructor and the students together in discussing the students' answers and the author's suggested answers to each thinking skills exercise. By their very nature the exercises can provoke different judgments and evaluations. This is not a weakness of the approach but a strength. It offers an opportunity, a springboard, to serious consideration of important skills that the historian uses in talking and writing about the past. Thus, the scene is set for stimulating discussion about the choices made in answering the exercises. This ensuing discussion further develops the students' thinking skills, enlivens the interaction between instructor and students, and encourages classroom discussion among the students. The students learn that historians have to make judgments, that they sometimes disagree, and that the neat and definite answers are not always possible in the study of and understanding of the past. Students learn to question the structuring and presentation of data both by the textbook and the instructor and the validity of evaluative and interpretive statements.

This Study Guide will be of practical use to the history instructor and to the students. The instructor can be assured that the students will, through the serious use of this guidebook, receive the thorough review of facts and ideas normally expected of a study guide. But also, the instructor can be confident that students are being introduced to critical thinking skills, trained in the use of reasoned judgment, and are, thus, going beyond the simple memorization of content as an end in itself.

Much of what I have developed in this guidebook, I owe not only to my many years of teaching and researching in history, but also to my four children who seemed constantly to employ critical thinking skills to challenge my judgments and evaluations, and to my wife, Keiko, whose Japanese frame of reference made me reexamine the whole process of critical thinking.

Dick Mumford

To the Student:
How to Use
This Study Guide

This Study Guide has many uses. Of course, it is a supplement to Joseph R. Conlin's textbook, *The American Past: A Survey of American History*, Fourth Edition, not a replacement. Narrative, descriptive history is very important for the study of history. It tells the story and describes the dramatic moments of the past. This particular textbook is especially rich in descriptive information and interesting, often unusual, sometimes fascinating, data. As in most texts, it is arranged in prose form—well structured sentences strung together in coherent paragraphs.

The Study Guide organizes material in a different design, it is analytical in approach. The emphasis is on processing data rather than only memorizing data. Ideas begin to sink in, to penetrate the mind, to excite awareness. You are asked to reflect, judge, evaluate, rank, decide, and distinguish. Your experience and judgment are made a part of the data of history, and the objective information is made subjective and internalized. The textbook supplies the data, the ideas, and the insight that are essential for understanding the history, and this Study Guide provides exercises for reviewing the text and for developing critical thinking skills. This book contains exercises to fulfill both purposes.

The first purpose of this book is to enable you, the student, to effectively review the text in preparation for quizzes and examinations. This book offers samples of true–false, multiple choice, completion, identification, and essay questions, as well as chronological exercises. In each case significant data and ideas are used that might conceivably appear on a test. Changing the false statements in the true–false exercise into true ones helps avoid the reinforcement of false data. Also, in many of the critical thinking skills exercises, filling in blanks with the correct words helps you think carefully about the fact or idea in the statement before placing the correct word in the blank.

To use this book to the best advantage you should read the text carefully before doing the exercises. When doing the exercises, read the statements and attempt to answer them correctly without referring to the answer key. In this way you effectively review the text and realize how well you have mastered it. If you cannot fill in the blanks correctly, return to the textbook for more study.

Chronological arrangements are also included at key spots where the *sequence* of events is important in understanding the topic. Thus, the basic review exercises found in all standard student workbooks are available and carefully designed for your use in the traditional manner.

Quantification has become a vital tool for the historian. If a picture is worth a thousand words, oftentimes a statistic is equal to at least a hundred words. A number offers more precision than the words *some, many, a few, quite, a large number,* or *a handful* used by historians. The use of statistical data has become essential for understanding nearly every textbook topic. Therefore, a special section of each chapter is devoted exclusively to an evaluation of statistical data from each textbook chapter. In order to challenge the memory and to provide a worthwhile review, these exercises require you to fill in blanks with the correct numbers. Then you must evaluate each statistical statement usually by judging its importance or by explaining whether it is understandable by itself or needs more data to be understood clearly. You not only learn the statistical data of importance but also begin to think about the data and to evaluate and judge it. A group of statistical data can be a most helpful way to perceive a topic; without relevant statistical data, knowledge of a subject remains vague and incomplete.

The concept/idea exercises help you formulate coherent answers for the short essay or what is often called "identification" topics. The concept section is very important for both preparing for examinations and developing synthesis skills. In these exercises ten or twelve key concepts or ideas are chosen from the chapter.. Other words, related to key concept in some way, are clustered beside it in parentheses. The object of the exercise is to identify the concept and show the relationship between it and the words. As a result, you will form the habit of thinking, not in terms of isolated, unrelated facts and unconnected data, but in a synthesis of facts all connected in some way to a single concept or idea. In forming relationships these exercises not only develop the skill of bringing together significant information but also carefully prepare you for the traditional short essay and "identify" questions on examinations. Furthermore, you are asked to determine whether the concept relates to a similar idea in other periods of history (present as well as past) or applies, primarily, in the period of history under consideration. Thus, ideas and data begin to make sense as your mind becomes active in learning rather than as only a passive receptor of processed knowledge. You begin to structure data in a meaningful, personal arrangement.

Most professors include essay questions on tests. This book offers several examples for each textbook chapter. These exercises call for, not a full essay, but an orderly presentation of factual material on a topic in the form of notes. Some questions require you to make judgments or offer a personal viewpoint. This controversial issue question, if approached thoughtfully and with the use of relevant factual evidence along with reasoned arguments, will impress your mind with data in such a way that you retain more data and organize it around an interesting and meaningful question or challenge. Thus you learn to pull in data, ideas, interpretations, and arguments around a core issue.

Beyond these more traditional uses of the Study Guide to understanding the text and reviewing for examinations, it is designed to encourage the development of critical thinking skills. Herein lies its uniqueness. Critical thinking is part of the daily practice of the historian as he or she reads, organizes, researches, and writes history. In this Study Guide you are not only introduced to thinking skills but are urged to practice these skills. Suggested answers are provided for such questions with which you may evaluate your own conclusions.

Some of the critical thinking skills that are important in studying history and are the focus of exercises in this book include the following:

1. Evaluation of Evidence: determining whether data is very relevant in understanding a topic or whether it is less relevant. *Very relevant* means that it is indispensable and essential in fully comprehending the topic.

2. Fact, Interpretation (or Evaluation, Judgment), or Opinion: determining whether a statement is factual (beyond serious question regarding its truth) or whether it is an interpretation. An interpretation is a professional viewpoint which the student might consider true and accurate but which is based upon an interpretation of facts, is derived or concluded from the data. An opinion is an expression of belief that does not have the weight of a professional's insight and is probably not based on methodical research.

3. Determining Importance: history scholars judge the importance of data by leaving out information that they consider unimportant. A significant part of historical thinking is deciding from among the mass of data those facts that are important enough to include in a book. This exercise requires you, in a limited way, to go through the same thinking process. From among a number of statements, you must distinguish between those of great and essential importance and those of lesser importance. You, therefore, function as a historian by choosing the important from the less important. This is a vital skill not only for the historian but also for anyone in society rapidly being overwhelmed by data.

4. Ranking: choosing the relative importance of a fact or idea related to other similar items in a group. These groups may also be causes of an event or the relative contributions of individuals or groups. Thus you must think, reflect, consider, and then decide on the relative importance of causes. This is similar to determining importance of data and ideas, but you must consider evidence to prove the value of one item in a group over other items.

5. Verifiable or Unverifiable: distinguishing between those statements for which there is very solid and perhaps unimpeachable evidence of its truth and accuracy and those statements that, although probably true and perhaps logical, cannot ultimately be verified because there are elements of opinion and interpretation integrated into the statement. You cannot always assume that any statement appearing in a history book is backed by extensive research and is indisputable.

Many other exercises of thinking skills are developed in particular chapters. Through these skills exercises, you can begin to understand these skills and integrate them in your study of history and in your overall thinking process.

Ideally, this book should be used as a basis for class discussion. You should compare your decisions and choices in the exercises with the answers in this book, with those of other students (preferably in a classroom setting), and with a discussion leader or professor. You should acquire the habit of making decisions and defending them with evidence and arguments against the views of other students. The answers to the thinking skills exercises are only "suggested answers," and you should feel free to disagree or question them. Too often in history classes, because the emphasis seems to be on facts coming from the lecture or text, students are reluctant to disagree, to argue, to challenge, or to express judgments based upon evidence or reasoned argument. This book invites you to learn actively, not passively.

The promise and expectation for this book is that, seriously and properly used, it becomes a vehicle for thorough review and a key to improved performance on examinations. Also, it promises to develop critical thinking skills that will not only result in better overall achievement in history courses, but also establish lasting habits of thought applicable to any situation.

The Research Paper

One of the major functions of historians is to research and write about the past. Nearly all historians consider it a primary responsibility and, perhaps, even the core of a definition of what it really means to be a historian. The thinking skills of the historian used in the process of research and writing are the same thinking skills that are encouraged in the exercises in this book. To "do history" is to do research by employing the historian's critical thinking skills.

Therefore, in many history classes the instructor will assign a research paper. Below are a list of guidelines designed to assist you through the process of research to a finished paper. The critical thinking skills developed by the serious use of this Study Guide should be of great assistance to your research and to the arrangement and writing of the final paper.

Some suggestions for research and writing history:

1. Choose a topic that is manageable, not too broad and general, and yet, not so narrow as to require source material not readily available.

2. Unless the professor has specific instructions on the research paper, orient the topic toward a question, issue, or a comparative study. If you choose only a topic, your paper is likely to turn out to be a patchwork of descriptions and the rewording of secondary sources without a meaningful thesis or direction.

3. Start immediately after the assignment is made—acquire books, find articles, read a general review of the issue or data related to the topic. This quick start serves two purposes. First, it allows you to think and plan the research paper at any spare moment. Also, it gives you time to change your mind and switch subjects if the first choice is unworkable.

4. Choose several questions related to the thesis of the paper—a type of rough outline of the direction of the paper.

5. Read and take notes on relevant data. If quotations are involved, quote precisely. Put on the note cards or notebook paper the full bibliographical information including the page number. This will avoid confusion when you pull ideas together in final form.

6. Divide your notecards according to subtopics. It is important to know when to stop taking notes and to start writing. Evidence can be collected "forever." so, a decision must be made as to when enough data is available to write the paper. There is no "golden moment" for writing. Do not wait. Write when you feel like it and when you *don't* feel like it. Avoid jargon and slang ("cart before the horse"). Use a variety of sentence structures—simple, complex, compound. Construct paragraphs around a topic and use an introductory sentence. Be concise and try to find the best way to say it, not just *a* way of saying it.

7. With a dictionary and thesaurus at hand and your note cards organized, write the paper section by section. Write double or triple space—on one side only. This gives you room to make changes between lines and on the reverse side. Of course, a word processor makes this operation easier.

8. In the introduction, explain what you are doing, the limitations of the paper, and the expected progression of the paper. Comment upon any difficulties in sources and point out the main effort of your work.

9. In a conclusion, summarize what you have proven and what you have not proven (that is, what more remains to be done). Relate, if possible, your conclusion to a broader spectrum—other historical periods or topics or similar issues at other times.

10. The historian's style is normally a statement, followed by evidence and arguments, and then evaluative statements about the relationship between the statement and the evidence. Reading aloud can help you refine style and smoothness. Use the active voice as much as possible.

11. Follow the bibliographical pattern required or suggested by your professor. Find out whether the professor requires footnotes (bottom of each page) or endnotes (at the end of the paper). Be careful to avoid plagiarism (taking another person's ideas or words without giving credit).

12. Proofread carefully. Have a friend read the paper also and offer comments or search for mistakes.

⚛1⚛

A Collision of Worlds

America and Europe
25,000 B.C. (?)–A.D. 1550

"War for the purpose of spreading their religion was holy, and ... death in such a war was a guarantee of salvation."

"That history is made by men and women is no longer denied except by some theologians and mystical metaphysicians."

I. **True–False**
If the statement is false, change any words necessary to make it true.

_____ 1. Some American Indian tribes wove reed and grass baskets so intricately that water could be stored in them.

_____ 2. Unlike other explorers, Columbus was actually looking for a New World in his voyages.

_____ 3. The Black Death (bubonic plague) killed about one-third of Europe's people.

_____ 4. The Roman Catholic Church taught that it was an act of piety to adorn cathedrals and chapels with beautiful or valuable objects.

_____ 5. Europeans rejoiced at the glories of Italy and the riches revealed in the Italian cathedrals.

_____ 6. The Ottoman subjugation of the Middle East increased the supply of goods entering Europe.

_____ 7. Portugal became even more interested in Columbus' plan to sail west to reach Asia after the voyage of Bartholomew Dias.

_____ 8. Cortez used Indian peoples who were resentful of Aztec domination to subdue Tenochtitlán.

_____ 9. The *Pinta*, one of Columbus' ships, could hold about as much in the way of supplies as a modern two-car garage.

_____ 10. Indians exposed to imported animals soon became dependent upon them.

II. Multiple Choice

_____ 1. Europeans brought to the New World
  a. tomatoes
  b. wheat
  c. beans
  d. manioc

_____ 2. What killed far more native Americans than Spanish swords or English muskets?
  a. agricultural labor
  b. warfare among the Indians
  c. deprivation of food
  d. bacteria and viruses

_____ 3. Which of the following is *not* a characteristic of the Aztec culture?
  a. worship of more than a thousand gods
  b. farming intensively
  c. use of a written language of 42 symbols
  d. building pyramid-shaped temples

_____ 4. To end the enslavement of Indians, de Las Casas advocated the
  a. importation of black Africans
  b. strict enforcement of church rules
  c. Indian conversion to Christianity
  d. Indian migration of Canada

_____ 5. Germany was not involved in the search for new trade routes because it was
  a. content to stay at home
  b. monopolizing trade in Europe
  c. still a patchwork of warring principalities
  d. at war with France

_____ 6. Columbus' plan for reaching the Indies by sailing west was based not on any pioneering breakthrough in geography but on
  a. his belief in Divine guidance
  b. a major error
  c. knowledge of Diaz' voyage
  d. his expertise in navigation

_____ 7. The Ottoman success in the Levant coincided with another important historical development, the
  a. discovery of the Indies
  b. arrival of incense in Europe
  c. victory of the Bantu in Nigeria
  d. revolution in agriculture

III. Quantification

Fill in each blank in the following statements with the correct number or numbers. Then determine whether you consider the statement to be very important (VI) or less important (LI). Write your choice in the blank to the left of each statement.

VI–LI

_____ 1. Columbus' ship, the *Pinta* could hold about as much in supplies as a _____ _____ _____ .

_____ 2. It is _____ miles from the Canary Islands to Japan. Columbus' estimate was _____ miles.

VI–LI

_____ 3. Cortez arrived on the Mexican mainland with _____ men and _____ horses.

_____ 4. Of _____ food crops grown in Africa today all but _____ originated in America.

_____ 5. About _____ million people died of syphilis in the Old World within _____ years of Columbus' voyage.

_____ 6. The Mayans built at least _____ cities in Meso-America with populations up to _____ each.

_____ 7. By 1500 native American languages numbered _____ .

_____ 8. Of the drugs and medicines in use in the United States today, _____ were known to the prehistoric Indians.

IV. Concepts–Ideas

Identify each of the following key words briefly and explain the relationship between them and the words that follow in parentheses. Then in the blank to the left indicate whether you think the concept has contemporary significance (CS) or is only significant in the past (PS). For those you have marked "CS," explain the contemporary connections, that is, in what way is the concept similar to events, ideas, and developments in modern times.

CS–PS

_____ 1. luxury goods (Spice Islands — tapestries — perfume — cinnamon — rich and powerful — decisions — risky)

_____

_____

_____ 2. brutish life (inequality — necessities— quality diet — clothing — housing — bathing — latrines)

_____

_____

_____ 3. status symbols (dyes— piety — incense — silk — gems — carpets — spices) EXAMPLE: We have status symbols today in yachts, expensive cars, beach houses, and so on.

_____

_____

_____ 4. Venetian wholesalers (middlemen — fleets — market towns — peddlers — expensive — donkey's back — toll — commission)

_____

_____

_____ 5. Meso-American (savage — gentle — intimate with nature — cities — books — gods — sacrifice — paralysis)

_____

_____

_____ 6. conquest (alliance — temples — marketplace — gods — gold — destroyed — lower class)

_____

_____ 7. *conquistadors* (fight — commerce —fanatic — religion — mercy — odds)

_____

_____ 8. Aztecs (1200s — invade — tribute — 6 square miles — London)

_____

_____ 9. Black Legend (cruel — killed — melted — demoralized — blacks — others — mixed blood)

_____

_____ 10. impact (cattle — ecology — horse — war — wool weaving — weeds — wheat — sugar cane)

_____

_____ 11. plant foods (corn — potato — China — West Africa — tomato — tobacco)

_____

_____ 12. microscopic life (smallpox — flu — viruses — syphilis — epidemics)

_____

V. Essay Questions

Write notes under each of the following questions that would help you answer similar essay questions on an exam.

1. What products did Europeans want from the East? Is the search for luxury a greater motivating force than the struggle for necessities? Why?

_____

_____

_____

2. Describe life in Europe before the discovery of the New World.

_____

_____

_____

3. What were the problems with the traditional trade items exchanged for the goods from Asia? Did the Levantine and Italian merchants actually damage their business with high profits? Explain.

_____

_____

_____

4. Explain the influence on Europe of the Turks and the revolution in agriculture. Which had the greater impact? Why?

_____

_____

_____

5. Describe the Portuguese and Spanish efforts to get to the East. How much does chance and coincidence play in the development of history (consider the efforts to get to the East)?

_____

_____

_____

6. Describe the struggle between the conquistadors and the Spanish. How should historians deal with moral issues such as the Spanish conquest of Mexico? Should historians condemn, excuse, or explain them?

_____

_____

_____

7. To what extent is the Black Legend deserved and to what extent is it an unfair label? Explain. Should you be critical of the Spanish or just accept it as the circumstances of the times?

_____

_____

_____

8. Evaluate the contributions of the Old World to the New World and of the New World to the Old World. Should the religious contribution be considered in the exchange? Why or why not?

_____

_____

_____

9. What was the life of the Mayan Indians like before the Age of Discovery? Be specific and detailed.

_____

_____

_____

10. Is it likely that another age of discovery and exploration will occur again? Why? What about the possibilities of space exploration?

_____

_____

_____

11. Should Columbus be considered a hero, a great man, a discoverer or should he be condemned for the destruction of native American civilizations? Explain why.

_____

_____

_____

VI. Motivation and Causation

The textbook at various places offers explanations of motivation and causation in discovery and exploration. Consider the items below and assign *each* a value from 1 to 5 depending on your interpretation of their importance as a factor of motivation and causation. A "5" would indicate a factor of great importance and a "1" would indicate a factor of very little importance in your judgment.

1–5

_____ a. Desire by the wealthy of Europe for luxury goods from the East.

_____ b. Accumulation of wealth by rulers who were then able to finance voyages of discovery.

_____ c. Failure of the crusades to break the Moslem control of the Holy Land (key trade connections for eastern goods.

_____ d. Resentment and envy by western European nations of Italian and Moslem wealth and control of products from the East.

_____ e. Success of Ottoman Turks in the Middle East—reduced the amount of goods transported through the area and limited eastern goods arriving in Europe.

_____ f. Revolution in agriculture produced more food, higher population, and a larger number of unemployed people looking for new opportunities.

_____ g. Powerful new governments (nation-states), centralized and wealthy, arose in Spain and Portugal.

_____ h. Change from a barter to a money economy increased the wealth of merchants who helped finance voyages.

_____ i. A taste for war and aggesssion instilled in the Portuguese and Spanish as a consequence of the long wars to drive the Moors from the Iberian Peninsula.

_____ j. The "explorers' institute" set up by Prince Henry the Navigator of mariners who studied geography and ship design and shared information.

_____ k. Both Spain and Portugal faced the Atlantic, had good ports, and looked to the future rather than back toward Europe and the past.

_____ l. The search for the Kingdom of Prester John in the 1400s and 1500s contributed to voyages of exploration.

_____ m. The courage, perseverance, bravery and skill of Bartholomew Diaz, Christopher Columbus, Vasco de Gama, Hernando Cortez, Francisco Pizarro, and other explorers.

_____ n. Columbus' error in calculation in which he judged Asia to be only 2,500 miles west of the Canary Islands.

_____ o. The greed for gold, silver, and other richess of the East and/or a New World.

_____ p. Spain's poor agricultural potential, the reluctance of aristocrats to engage in commerce, and their preference for fighting and adventure.

_____ q. The religious faith of the Spaniards, their belief in a holy war for assured salvation, and their religious belief that nonbelievers had no rights and could be exploited.

VII. Questions

Refer to your answers in the previous "Motivation and Causation" exercise in answering the following questions.

1. Did your assignment of a value to each item move in the direction of economic factors, political/diplomatic causes, or personal/human reasons? Is this a matter of principle by which you judge causes for many events or does it apply only in this case? Explain.

_____

_____

_____

2. For the two items that you gave the highest rank, explain why you consider them the most important.

   a. _____

   _____

   _____

   b. _____

   _____

   _____

3. For the two items that you gave the lowest rank, explain why you consider them the least important.

a. _____

_____

_____

b. _____

_____

_____

4. Can you think of any other causes of motivations that are not included in the list? Explain these.

_____

_____

_____

VIII. Fact–Judgment

Determine whether you consider each of the following statements to be a fact (F) or a judgment (J). A judgment may be true and you may agree with it, but it remains a judgment because it is *derived from* fact and not a fact itself. It could be either a reasoned judgment or a professional interpretation. Write your choice in the blank to the left of the statement.

F–J

_____ 1. To our knowledge, Mayan hieroglyphics is the only writing system developed in America.

_____ 2. Untold numbers of European, Japanese, and Chinese fishermen were probably blown off course and made a landfall in the Western Hemisphere.

_____ 3. In Europe at the time of Columbus, the wealthiest of the population controlled and consumed far more than their share of goods and resources.

_____ 4. Spices enhanced food taste, were preservatives, and were believed to have medicinal value.

_____ 5. Resentment and envy gave birth to the dream of finding a new route to the source of precious Eastern goods.

_____ 6. In 1453 the Ottoman Turks captured Constantinople and by 1529 they reached the gates of Vienna.

_____ 7. Improved plows, the use of horses over oxen, and the emphasis on sheep raising meant fewer people were needed to produce food and thus many from rural areas lacked employment.

_____ 8. Had he known the correct size of the earth, Columbus might have abandoned his scheme.

_____ 9. The Aztecs, who practiced human sacrifice, tearing out, cooking and eating human hearts, were a disgusting people.

_____ 10. Perhaps no people were so well suited by their history for conquest as the Spanish because they shunned commerce and lived in a land unsuited to agriculture.

_____ 11. After Pizarro killed the ruler of the Incas, the morale of the people collapsed.

_____ 12. The Spaniards were no more brutal or ruthless than any conquering people would have been, given the same opportunities.

_____ 13. The crops contributed by the New World to the Old World were of more value than those brought to the New World by the Old.

_____ 14. The most tragic exchange between the hemispheres was in the microscopic forms of life.

_____ 15. Sugar cane was the most valuable crop brought to America from Europe.

IX. Lessons and Generalizations

Listed below are some lessons of history and generalizations about history. Write in the space before each of these whether you think they are valid (V), partially valid in some cases (P), or invalid (I).

_____ 1. Often the effort to overcome an evil in society, unless carefully scrutinized for consequences, can result in the development of another evil. (The monk, de La Casas, received the Spanish King's permission to start the African slave trade in order to save the Indians from extermnination.)

_____ 2. The unforeseen consequences of any action are too often greater than the intended consequences. (Columbus sought a way to the East and found a new world. The Ottoman Turks reduced the flow of goods to Europe and thus spawned the search around Africa and across the Atlantic, which ended the need for Middle East trade.)

_____ 3. Increased population is a disruptive force in history. (It leads to expansion, unemployment, and wars).

_____ 4. Those people with superiority in military technology, even if they have disadvantages in numbers and location, will defeat those with inferior military technology. (The Spanish defeated the Aztecs and Incas.)

_____ 5. In trade, discovery, or any new interaction between peoples, aspects such as technology, plants, animals, and diseases are more important than the political and military.

_____ 6. That which seems proper, correct, moral and just in one period of history may be considered brutal, immoral, intolerant, and reproachful at another time in history. (How did the Spanish behave in Mexico and Peru—consider the view at the time and the view today.)

_____ 7. All developments of history are a mixed bag of good and evil, benevolence and harm, short-run turmoil for long-run benefits. (The Spanish mistreated the Indians, yet established two universities; intermarriage brought an end to the continued Indian warfare; gold and silver from the New World was used to finance religious wars in Europe; destructive diseases spread both ways across the Atlantic, yet numerous useful plants and animals were also exchanged.)

ANSWERS

I. True–False
1. True
2. False
3. True
4. True
5. False
6. False
7. False
8. True
9. True
10. True

II. Multiple Choice
1. b
2. d
3. c
4. a
5. c
6. b
7. d

III. Quantification
LI 1. two-car garage
VI 2. 9,000; 2,500
VI 3. 300; 18
VI 4. 640; 50
VI 5. 10; 15
LI 6. 40; 20,000
VI 7. 500
LI 8. 230

IV. Concepts–Ideas
1. PS
2. PS
3. CS
4. PS
5. CS
6. CS
7. CS
8. PS
9. CS
10. CS
11. PS
12. CS

VIII. Fact–Judgment
1. F
2. J
3. J
4. F
5. J
6. F
7. F
8. J
9. J
10. J
11. J
12. J
13. J
14. J
15. J

England Goes to America

The Struggle to Plant a Colony, 1550–1624

"Hark, hark, the dogs do bark;
The beggars are coming to town."

"God's breath dispersed a hostile
fleet"

I. True–False

If the statement is false, change any words necessary to make it true.

_____ 1. A buffer zone between the Plymouth and London companies was designed to avoid the kind of rivalries that had sometimes turned violent in the Spanish colonies.

_____ 2. The longest lasting English trading company was the Levant Company.

_____ 3. In the 1500s in England a person could be hanged for stealing a loaf of bread.

_____ 4. Children were an economic liability in America.

_____ 5. Sugar was the most important product in the West Indies.

_____ 6. The Spanish ships were too small in the Armada's struggle against the British in 1588.

_____ 7. The settlers of the Roanoke Island colony migrated to Florida to found St. Augustine.

_____ 8. At least in part, Pope Clement VIII refused to grant Henry VIII's divorce because he feared the power of the Spanish king.

_____ 9. The habit of "drinking" tobacco spread steadily throughout Europe.

_____ 10. Virginia was granted a House of Burgesses (legislative assembly) that would elect a governor.

II. Multiple Choice

_____ 1. In 1500 the Church owned about how much of the land in Europe?

    a. one-half
    b. one-tenth
    c. one-third
    d. one-thirtieth

_____ 2. Sir Walter Raleigh considered colonies in North America primarily as

    a. naval bases for privateers
    b. sources of food and textiles
    c. havens for criminals and the poor
    d. sources of future taxes for the monarchy

_____ 3. The enclosure movement

    a. substituted wheat growing for sheep herding
    b. established stone fences around the few remaining forests of England
    c. was the British strategy for defeating Spain
    d. turned cultivated lands into sheep runs

_____ 4. A goal of mercantilism was to

    a. export more than import
    b. import more than export
    c. let other nations carry products
    d. bring timber and naval stores from Russia

_____ 5. In reality, America did offer hope to the English because

    a. familiar crops grew in America
    b. there were no laws against poaching
    c. there was plenty of wood for fires
    d. all of the above
    e. only a and c

_____ 6. The odds were that a person who survived the childhood diseases of the sixteenth century would die before the age of

    a. 55
    b. 70
    c. 35
    d. 20

_____ 7. The system that granted each person or head of a household 50 acres of land in Virginia was called the

    a. homestead plan
    b. headright system
    c. indenturing
    d. land control system

III. Quantification

Fill in each blank in the following statements with the correct number or numbers. Then determine whether you consider the statement to be very important (VI) or less important (LI). Write your choice in the blank to the left of each statement.

VI–LI

_____ 1. Francis Drake's voyage around the world for Elizabeth I brought profits of _____ percent in Spanish treasure.

_____ 2. In 1500 the Church owned about _____ of the land in Europe.

_____ 3. Spain enjoyed a monopoly in the New World for _____ .

_____ 4. Luther presented _____ arguments attacking doctrines and practices of the Church in 1517.

_____ 5. A population of over _____ men and women was reduced to _____ in the winter of 1609–10 in Virginia.

_____ 6. By 1618 in Virginia one industrious man could tend _____ tobacco plants and _____ acres of maize, beans and squash—enough to feed _____ people.

_____ 7. The "headright system" enabled a person to receive _____ acres of land for himself and _____ acres for every other person whose passage he paid.

_____ 8. In 1622 the Powhatan Indians, under the leadership of Opechaneanough, attacked Jamestown killing _____ whites, perhaps _____ of Virginia's population.

_____ 9. Depending on winds and currents, a sailing ship made the trip between England and the colonies in anywhere from _____ weeks to _____ months.

IV. Concepts–Ideas

Identify each of the following key words briefly and explain the relationship between them and the words that follow in the parentheses.

1. *siglo de oro* (Spanish power — preoccupied France and England — 100 years)

_____

_____

2. "theses" (attack doctrines and practices — charismatic Luther — princes and Church lands)

_____

_____

3. survivor (Protestant, Catholic, Protestant — neither yes or no — say nothing)

_____

_____

4. Drake (Sea Dog — Spanish treasure — knighted — circumnavigation)

_____

_____

5. promotion (Raleigh lobbies — riches — letters — hope — fires, game, and crops)

_____

_____

6. curse of Spanish gold (bottome of mines — purchase abroad — imports — elegance)

_____

_____

7. gold and wealth (exports over imports — transport goods — colonies for resources — self-sufficient)

_____

_____

8. enclosure movement (excess population — hedges — wool over wheat — labor reduced — beggars)

_____

_____

9. "bloody code" (maintain social order — ship to colonies — safety valve — wretched poor)

_____

_____

10. joint stock company (venture capital — shares — charter — monopoly — London Company)

_____

_____

11. "noxious weed" ("miracle drug" — Rolfe — slaves — soaring economy)

_____

_____

12. headright (50 acres — indentured servants — land attraction)

_____

_____

13. crews ("shanghaiing" — choices — alluring opportunity — brutal and short)

_____

_____

14. seamen (battles — executions — scurvy — food — work)

_____

_____

15. massacre (trade items — ancestral lands — superior weapons)

_____

_____

V. Essay Questions

Write notes under each of the following questions that would help you answer similar essay questions on an exam.

1. Describe the massacre of 1622. Were the colonists justified in expanding into the hunting land of the Indians and were the Indians justified in attacking Jamestown? Should the word massacre be used or should we say that the Indians defended their homelands? Explain.

_____

_____

2. What were the important features of the indentured servant system? Was it a "golden opportunity" for the poor to seek a better life in the New World or was it a system of legal exploitation of the poor by the upper class? Why?

_____

_____

3. Describe the method of financing and sponsoring colonization. Did the private enterprise approach result in success over obstacles and thus turn out to be the most effective method of colonization or was it cruel and exploitative, causing needless suffering that could have been alleviated by more government support and direction? Explain.

_____

_____

4. Explain the economic system of mercantilism. Would mercantilism work in the world today? Why or why not? What features are still with us in contemporary economies?

_____

_____

5. Sir Francis Drake was knighted by Elizabeth I. Should he be considered a pirate or terrorist in contemporary judgment? Why?

_____

_____

6. Explain the developments of the Protestant Reformation. Some people argue that Luther, the German princes, and English reformers had important religious reasons for leaving the Catholic Church. Others maintain that economic and political factors in Europe and the divorce issue

coupled with rich monastery lands in England caused the Reformation. How do you react to this debate?

_____

_____

7. Would you consider Elizabeth I a wise monarch who had political insight and practical common sense or an opportunist, unprincipled, deceitful monarch who knighted pirates and encouraged plunder?

_____

_____

8. What were the reasons for the English decision to colonize America? List and explain briefly. Was the economic motivation strongest or was it one reason among many? Explain.

_____

_____

9. Explain the economic difficulties suffered by Spain in spite of the gold and silver received from the New World. Are there nations today who have great wealth and resources but do not seem to progress? Explain.

_____

_____

10. Write an essay on common seamen in the seventeenth and eighteenth centuries.

_____

_____

_____

VI. Ranking

Rank the following people or groups from 1 to 10 according to your assessment of their importance in the English settlement of the New World. The most important would be 1, and the least important would be 10. Then answer the following questions.

1–10

_____ a. Martin Luther

_____ b. Elizabeth I

_____ c. Sir Walter Raleigh

_____ d. Sir Francis Drake

_____ e. London Company stockholders

_____ f. colonial promoters

_____ g. wealthy English landholders

_____ h. Lord de La Warr

_____ i. John Rolfe

_____ j. Thomas Mun

1. For the two choices you gave the highest rank, explain why you consider them the most important.

   a. _____

   _____

   _____

   b. _____

   _____

   _____

2. For the choice you gave the lowest rank, explain why you consider it the least important.

   _____

   _____

   _____

3. What criteria or standards did you use in making your choices? What specific characteristics or action did you consider important?

   _____

   _____

   _____

VII. Motivation

Rank from 1 to 8 the following list of motivations that encouraged English settlement in the New World. The most important would be 1 and the least important would be 8.

1–8

_____ a. Population increase—North America provided a safety valve for increased population and the accompanying unemployment.

_____ b. Mercantilism—the accepted economic principles of the time that a nation needed colonies to supply natural resources and purchase manufactured goods.

_____ c. The desire by merchants for profits through joint-stock company enterprises.

_____ d. The dream of a better life, the promise of the New World as a land of opportunity—pictured as such by promoters.

_____ e. Desire for land by those who had enough money to meet the headright requirement of passage.

_____ f. Severe conditions in England due to the enclosure movement, high unemployment and a severe criminal code.

_____ g. Political ambition of the monarch for glory, power, and wealth as well as a way of ridding the nation of nonconformists.

_____ h. National competition and rivalry with the Dutch and the Spanish—desire to protect the nation by gaining economic power and control of the Atlantic.

1. For the two choices you gave the highest rank, explain why you consider them the most important.

    a. _____

    _____

    _____

    b. _____

    _____

    _____

2. Use your imagination—are there other causes besides these eight? Speculate!

_____

_____

_____

VIII. Fact–Judgment

Determine whether you consider each of the following statements to be a fact (F) or a judgment (J). A judgment may be true and you may agree with it, but it remains a judgment because it is *derived from* fact and not a fact itself. It could be either a reasoned judgment or a professional interpretation. Write your choice in the blank to the left of the statement.

F–J

_____ 1. The common people had long been disgusted with the moral laxity of many priests and resented the fact that the Church owned about one-third of the land in Europe.

_____ 2. In 1527 Henry VIII of England rejected the pope's authority and declared himself head of the Church of England.

_____ 3. The simple act of striking down an ancient and powerful authority produced a spirit of religious debate and innovation.

_____ 4. Philip II claimed all of North America for Spain, but the northermost outpost was in Florida.

_____ 5. Sir Walter Raleigh did more than any other individual to stimulate English interest in the possibilities of colonization.

_____ 6. So crushing was the Armada's defeat that the English could be excused for claiming that God was on their side.

_____ 7. By 1600 there were plenty of signs that Spain's American gold and silver mines were as much a curse as a blessing.

_____ 8. The bulk of the vaunted Spanish army was imported from abroad as German mercenaries.

_____ 9. England's population increased from 3 to 4 million in the sixteenth century while food production did not keep pace.

_____ 10. The personal losses of Gilbert and Raleigh persuaded English merchants that the joint-stock company was the medium for making money out of America.

_____ 11. The investors in London never did realize a profit on their enterprise in America.

_____ 12. The first black Americans were almost certainly not slaves but were sold into servitude for a specific term.

ANSWERS

I. True–False	II. Multiple Choice	III. Quantification	VIII. Fact–Judgment
1. True	1. c	VI 1. 4,700	1. J
2. False	2. a	VI 2. one-third	2. F
3. True	3. d	LI 3. 100	3. J
4. False	4. a	LI 4. 95	4. F
5. True	5. d	LI 5..500; 60	5. J
6. False	6. c	LI 6. 2,000; 4; 5	6. J
7. False	7. b	VI 7. 50; 50	7. J
8. True		VI 8. 350; one-quarter	8. F
9. True		VI 9. 6; 3	9. F
10. False			10. J
			11. F
			12. F

Puritans and Proprietors

The Growth of Colonial America
1620–1732

" … lump of wretchedness … a city on a hill … a scold."

"The best use of history as an innoculation against radical expectations, and hence embittering disappointments."

George Will

I. True–False
If the statement is false, change any words necessary to make it true.

_____ 1. Governor Stuyvesant wanted to surrender New York to the British because he did not get along with the New Netherlanders.

_____ 2. The Pilgrims disapproved of the Church of England, but they were English to the core.

_____ 3. Governor William Bradford took farmland from individual families and established a communal arrangement in Plymouth.

_____ 4. The Puritans intended to create a Godly Commonwealth such as the earth had never quite known.

_____ 5. The Puritans believed that men and women could earn salvation by acts of faith and charity.

_____ 6. Puritan life was closely relgulated because the Puritans believed that if they tolerated sin among themselves they would be punished.

_____ 7. Roger Williams encouraged the English to settle in America over the objections of the Indians.

_____ 8. Connecticut and Yale University were founded because Thomas Hooker and his followers believed that the Puritans of Massachusetts Bay and the faculty of Harvard were too lax and not strict enough.

_____ 9. Catholics in Maryland were trusted and respected as leaders by the non-Catholic majority.

_____ 10. The Dutch contributed cole slaw, the coddling of children, and several words such as "fun" and "hanky-panky" to American culture.

_____ 11. Pietists from the German Rhineland and from Switzerland settled in Lancaster and York counties in Pennsylvania.

_____ 12. The Carolinas by 1700 raised tobacco and food products primarily.

II. Multiple Choice

_____ 1. The Society of Friends did *not* believe in

    a. pacifism
    b. toleration of other religious beliefs
    c. deference to authority by removing hats and addressing important people with respectful words
    d. equality of women

_____ 2. Anne Hutchinson did *not*

    a. criticize the most distinguished preacher of Massachusetts
    b. teach that a spiritual individual could be raised above civil authority
    c. organize groups to discuss Sunday sermons
    d. agree that Winthrop and preachers could determine who could be admitted to church membership

_____ 3. The Puritans believed that

    a. social class and social distinctions were divinely decreed
    b. other religious groups should be tolerated
    c. the Sabbath was like any other day
    d. people could freely choose their eternal destiny

_____ 4. Democracy is not a fit government for church or commonwealth. This statement would be approved by

    a. William Penn
    b. John Cotton
    c. Roger Williams
    d. James Oglethorpe

_____ 5. Religious toleration was practiced the *least* in

    a. Pennsylvania
    b. New Jersey
    c. Massachusetts
    d. Rhode Island

_____ 6. In Puritan New England both incest and homosexuality were considered

    a. acceptable in private
    b. capital crimes
    c. punishable by fine and prison
    d. signs of the end times

III. Quantification

Fill in each blank in the following statements with the correct number or numbers. Then determine whether you consider the statement to be clear (C) or ambiguous (A) and whether it is very important (VI) or less important (LI). Write your choices in the blanks to the left of the statement.

C–A   VI–LI

_____   _____   1. During the first winter _____ of the 102 original colonists at Plymouth died of malnutrition or disease.

_____   _____   2. Of the 102 who founded Plymouth, only _____ were church members.

_____   _____   3. Between 1630 and 1640, _____ people left England for Massachusetts.

_____   _____   4. By the time of the American Revolution in 1776, _____ of the thirteen colonies were royal colonies.

_____   _____   5. The Van Renssaelerwyck estate south of Albany, New York, consisted of _____ acres.

_____   _____   6. King Charles II gave Pennsylvania to William Penn, the son of a man to whom the king owed _____ pounds.

_____   _____   7. The Aldens of Plymouth had more than _____ great-grandchildren.

IV. Concepts–Ideas

Identify each of the following key words briefly and explain the relationship between them and the related words that follow in parentheses. Then in the blank to the left indicate whether you think the concept has contemporary significance (CS) or is only significant in the past (PS). For those you have marked "CS," explain the contemporary connections, that is, in what way is the concept similar to events, ideas, and developments in modern times.

CS–PS

_____   1.   Pilgrim (traveler —English — worship —Mayflower —choice of worship —communal —compact —democratic)

_____

_____

_____   2.   Puritan (ready-made city — Godly Commonwealth — charter — human nature — grace — Elect — covenant)

_____

_____

_____   3.   mission ("city on a hill" — regulated — victimless crime — community)

_____

_____

_____   4.   "Blue Laws" (Sunday — "idle chatter" — nagging — stocks — death penalty — adultery — social class)

_____

_____

_____ 5. conscience (zealous — rigorous — Indian title — charter— toleration — saint or not)

_____

_____

_____ 6. "Antinomianism" (study word — woman — mental balance — direct spirit — Indians)

_____

_____ 7. feudal (proprietary — vice — kings — headrights — quitrent — small — wheat — tobacco — arrowheads)

_____

_____

_____ 8. Dutch (land — church — language — cole slaw — folklore — coddle — fun)

_____

_____

_____ 9. holy experiment (pacifism — inner light — social class — oaths — thee, thy, thou — women — toleration)

_____

_____

_____ 10. philanthropy (fortress colony — imprison for debt — "trust" — small landholdings — no slavery — no alcohol — disgust)

_____

_____

V. Essay Questions

Write notes under each of the following questions that would help you answer similar essay questions on an exam.

1. List the main features of Puritan theology and explain each feature briefly. What makes it distinct and different? Explain.

_____

_____

2. Examine the foundation and building of all the colonies and then point out the economic factors that were influential in this process of settling. Was the dominant reason for settlement economic or religious? Why?

_____

_____

_____

3. Describe the major individuals who were instrumental in founding colonies. Then choose the one who most impresses you and explain your choice.

_____

_____

_____

4. Was the diversity of the English colonies beneficial or harmful to their development and prosperity? Explain. Be specific.

_____

_____

_____

5. What features of the Puritans made them suitable to establish successful colonies in a New World?

_____

_____

_____

6. Describe the process of settlement by the Puritans at Plymouth. Do they deserve such an important symbolic place in American history? Why or why not?

_____

_____

_____

7. Was "Merrymount" ever a possibility in America? Why? How might development of New England have been different if it had been successful?

_____

_____

_____

8. Explain the beliefs of Roger Williams and Anne Hutchinson. Are they to be praised for their independence or criticized for their threat to a struggling community in the wilderness? Explain.

_____

_____

_____

9. What are the similarities and differences in the founding and development of Maryland and of Pennsylvania? Be specific. Which was a more desirable place to live? Why?

_____

_____

_____

10. Compare Anne Bradstreet and Anne Hutchinson. In what ways were they similar and in what ways different? Which do you admire more? Why?

_____

_____

_____

11. Explain how the Puritans were not "Puritans."

_____

_____

_____

VI. Ranking

Rank the following people or groups from 1 to 7 according to your assessment of their importance to the foundation of American society—their influence on the character, beliefs, and attitudes which we call American. The most important would be 1, and the least important would be 7.

1–7

_____ a. James Oglethorpe

_____ b. William Penn

_____ c. Quakers

_____ d. George Calvert

1–7

_____ e. John Winthrop

_____ f. Roger Williams

_____ g. Pilgrims

1. Explain why you ranked your first choice as the most important.

_____

_____

_____

2. Explain why you ranked your seventh choice as the least important.

_____

_____

_____

VII. Verifiable—Unverifiable—Significance

Determine whether each of the following statements is verifiable (V) or unverifiable (U) and whether it is very significant (VS) in understanding settlement or less significant (LS). Write your answers in the blanks to the left of the statement.

V–U   VS–LS

_____ _____ 1. England did not permit subjects to travel abroad without permission.

_____ _____ 2. New England life would have developed differently if the anarchic attitude of William Morton had continued.

V–U VS–LS

___ ___ 3. The Mayflower Compact, which assumed the authority of the government derived from some of the people, had great democratic potential.

___ ___ 4. The Puritans were a powerful minority in England and they worshipped as they pleased there.

___ ___ 5. The refusal of the Separatists in England to attend services of the Church of England was a crime.

___ ___ 6. The lawbooks of the New England colonies were filled with regulations that, in the late twentieth century, would be considered outrageous and ridiculous.

___ ___ 7. One early governor of New Hampshire married a widow of ten days.

___ ___ 8. The Quakers worried the authorities because of their Christian pacifism.

___ ___ 9. The society at Charleston was cultured and cosmopolitan, quite obnoxious to the democratic small farmers of the north.

___ ___ 10. Pennsylvania was the most cosmopolitan and liberal-minded colony in English America.

___ ___ 11. At the time, the Quakers were thought of much as later generations would think of "Holy Rollers," "Moonies," or "Hare Krishnas."

___ ___ 12. Anne Bradstreet's love lyrics, descriptions of the Massachusetts landscape, and variations on Puritan religious beliefs raised her far above any American contemporary.

ANSWERS

I. True–False	II. Multiple Choice	III. Quantification	IV. Concepts–Ideas	VII. Verifiable-Unverifiable-Significance
1. False	1. c	C LI 1. 44	1. PS	1. V VS
2. True	2. d	A VI 2. 35	2. PS	2. U VS
3. False	3. a	C VI 3. 21,000	3. CS	3. U VS
4. True	4. b	A LI 4. 9	4. CS	4. U VS
5. False	5. c	C LI 5. 700,000	5. CS	5. V VS
6. True	6. b	C VI 6. 16,000	6. CS	6. U LS
7. False		A LI 7. 400	7. PS	7. V LS
8. True			8. PS	8. U LS
9. False			9. CS	9. U VS
10. True			10. CS	10. U LS
11. True				11. U LS
12. False				12. U LS

4

Colonial Society:

English Legacies and Laws, American Facts of Life

"Thou shalt not suffer a witch to live."

"God sifted a whole Nation that He might send choice grain into the wilderness."

William Stoughton

I. True–False

The first statement is true. The second sentence is either true or false and related to the first. If the second statement is false, change any words necessary to make it true.

_____ 1. New Englanders bought slaves in West Africa and traded this merchandise in the West Indies for molasses, which was taken to New England to be made into rum. Profit was made only on the exchange of rum for slaves.

_____ 2. From England the southern colonies imported cheap clothing, shoes, and tools and many luxuries for the planter class. These colonies fit in well with the mercantilist system.

_____ 3. The colonists responded to the low price of tobacco by importing more black slaves and by engaging in illegal trade-smuggling. Evasion of the Navigation Acts was difficult because of the topography of the Chesapeake country.

_____ 4. The middle class of the tobacco colonies lived across the ocean. The ships transporting tobacco took the banks, factories, and commercial apparatus with them to sea.

_____ 5. The crops that New England produced—grain, livestock, beans, and fruits—were the same as those which flourished in England. Thus English mercantilists took less interest in New England than in the South.

_____ 6. Each year's sub-zero winter in New England heaved more boulders to the surface of the earth. The requirement of intense labor and rocky soil led New Englanders to import their food.

_____ 7. Witchcraft was mentioned in the Bible along with the admonition "Thou shalt not suffer a witch to live." Hardly anyone, except those in remote, backward areas, believed in witchcraft in the seventeenth century.

_____ 8. In New York, in theory, only the Church of England was legal. However, the laws were rarely enforced.

_____ 9. Foodstuffs (with the exception of rice) were not enumerated under the Navigation Acts. Thus they could be sold wherever the sellers could find a market.

_____ 10. The "Pennsylvania Dutch" are not really Dutch but are descended from German immigrants. They were called Dutch because the German word for "German" is Deutsch.

II. Multiple Choice

_____ 1. The Yankee merchants of New England did all but

   a. dodge British trade laws
   b. disregard directions from Cromwell and Parliament
   c. refuse to acknowledge the King
   d. claim they were members of the Church of England

_____ 2. Which of the following was *not* an aspect of the witchcraft trials of 1692 in the village of Salem?

   a. a general belief in witchcraft at the time
   b. young girls fell ill with fits of screaming
   c. people who expressed doubt were automatically added to those accused
   d. no one was actually hanged as a witch

_____ 3. Which of the following suffered as a result of the 1688 "Glorious Revolution" in England?

   a. the Penn family
   b. merchants of New England
   c. Jacob Leisler
   d. the Calverts of Maryland

_____ 4. Southern plantation life included

   a. a mansion in the style of an English manor
   b. port and Madeira wines
   c. rounds of dinners, parties, balls
   d. education at Oxford, Cambridge, or William and Mary
   e. all of the above

_____ 5. The first state university was established in

   a. North Carolina
   b. Massachusetts
   c. Virginia
   d. New Jersey

_____ 6. Nathaniel Bacon forced the governor to flee Virginia and governed Virginia for several months until he died by

   a. execution
   b. dueling
   c. disease
   d. accident

_____ 7. English farmers (in England) were forbidden to plant

   a. indigo
   b. tobacco
   c. maize or corn
   d. rice

III. Quantification

Fill in each blank in the following statements with the correct number or numbers. Then determine whether you consider the statement to be very important (VI) or less important (LI). Place your choice in the blank to the left of each statement.

VI–LI

_____ 1. By 1702, there were _____ British subjects in North America.

_____ 2. In 1629, _____ members of the Virginia assembly had been indentured servants five years earlier.

_____ 3. In 1692, _____ witches were hanged in Salem and another was pressed to death.

_____ 4. If a Puritan sermon lasted less than _____ hours, there might be gossip about the preacher's lack of zeal.

_____ 5. Charles II collected £ _____ a year from the tax on tobacco alone.

IV. Concepts–Ideas

Identify each of the following key words briefly and explain the relationship between them and the words that follow in parentheses.

1. enumerated articles (England only —world market products)

_____

_____

2. smuggling (evasion — bribery)

_____

_____

3. aggressive policy (tame tribes — stockades — prosperous trade)

_____

_____

4. cities afloat (banks — factories — middle class — London)

_____

_____

5. indebtedness (anti-British — tobacco merchants — luxury)

_____

_____

6. "Yankee Trader" (shrewdness — codfish — ingenious accommodations)

_____

_____

7. black magic (supernatural — not suffer witch to live — servants of Devil)

_____

_____

8. balanced economies (small farms — "breadbasket" — livestock)

_____

_____

9. meeting house (clapboard — Church of Rome — preach and worship — weathercock)

_____

_____

10. rice plantation (cash crop — intensive — mosquitoes — indigo)

_____

_____

V. Essay Questions

Write notes under each of the following questions that would help you answer similar essay questions on an exam.

1. Describe the witchcraft trials at Salem in 1792 and explain why you think they took place.

_____

_____

_____

2. Compare and contrast the economy and style of life in New England with that of the southern colonies. Point out specific similarities and differences.

_____

_____

_____

3. In which area of the colonies would you have preferred to live as a member of the upper class? Explain why.

_____

_____

_____

4. What features and developments in this colonial period led to or helped bring about the American Revolution? Be specific.

_____

_____

_____

5. List and explain briefly the Navigation Acts. Were British trade regulations oppressive and unfair or were they reasonable and beneficial? Explain. Be specific.

_____

_____

_____

6. Describe the differences and antagonisms between the tidewater and the Piedmont. What were the issues in Bacon's Rebellion?

_____

_____

_____

7. What is meant by a "land without cities"? Was the South at a disadvantage in not having cities? Why or why not?

_____

_____

_____

8. Describe the planters' style of life in Virginia, Maryland, and the Carolinas. Did this predetermine the future of southern society? Why or why not?

_____

_____

_____

9. Explain the British efforts in establishing the Dominion of New England. Would this have worked if the Glorious Revolution had not occurred in England? Why or why not?

_____

_____

_____

10. What was a typical Sunday like for the Puritans? Why do you think that this style of life broke down in later generations?

_____

_____

_____

VI. Significance of Data

Determine whether each of the following statements is very significant (VS) or less significant (LS). Write your choice in the blank to the left of the statement.

VS–LS

_____ 1. The British Empire was established in a fit of absent-mindedness with much disorganization and unclear regulation.

_____ 2. All goods going to the colonies from Europe had to go to England first, and there be unloaded and reloaded for shipment to America.

_____ 3. Governor Berkeley of Virginia was involved in a prosperous trade with the Indians, exchanging English goods for furs and deerskins.

_____ 4. In October 1676 Nathaniel Bacon fell ill with malaria and died, thus ending the largest rebellion in the American colonies.

_____ 5. The middle class of the tobacco colonies lived across the ocean in European cities where the banks, factories, and commercial apparatus were centered.

_____ 6. Sailors spent money for games and drinks at the private wharves of Virginia planters.

_____ 7. South Carolina planters spent their time in Charleston while overseers managed their plantations.

_____ 8. In New England, each year's sub-zero winter heaved boulders to the surface which had to be removed before plowing.

_____ 9. The word "Yankee" probably came from the Dutch word for "Johnny" or Janke.

_____ 10. New England colonies in the 1600s functioned much like independent commonwealths, even minting their own money.

_____ 11. Most of the Salem witchcraft victims were women without friends.

_____ 12. The Middle Colonies' agricultural pattern was a patchwork of small, family farms tilled by the owners themselves.

_____ 13. Many people took notes on the sermons of Puritan preachers.

_____ 14. For the Puritans on the Sabbath there would be no cooking, no work, no play, and no sports; even conversation was sparse.

_____ 15. Newport, Rhode Island, was a center of the African slave trade.

ANSWERS

I. True–False	II. Multiple Choice	III. Quantification	VI. Significance of Data
1. False	1. c	VI 1. 300,000	1. VS
2. True	2. d	VI 2. 7	2. VS
3. False	3. c	LI 3. 19	3. LS
4. True	4. e	LI 4. 2	4. LS
5. True	5. a	VI 5. 100,000	5. VS
6. False	6. c		6. LS
7. False	7. b		7. LS
8. True			8. VS
9. True			9. LS
10. True			10. VS
			11. LS
			12. LS
			13. LS
			14. LS
			15. LS

⟞5⟝

The Other Americans

The Indians, French, and Africans of Colonial North America

" ... where the English come to settle, a Divine hand makes way for them, by removing or cutting off the Indians either by Wars one with another, or by some raging mortal Disease."
Daniel Danton

"To take no sides in history would be as false as to take no sides in life."
Barbara Tuchman

I. True–False
If the statement is false, change any words necessary to make it true.

_____ 1. The English had little interest in conquering, living among, exploiting, and governing the native peoples.

_____ 2. None of the Indians worshipped only one god; none were monotheists.

_____ 3. Among the Indians themselves, the linguistic differences were greater than they were among the various nationalities of Europe.

_____ 4. Foraging for food gave secure livelihood to the Indians and helped them grow in size.

_____ 5. The English (and Dutch and French) desire for furs and hides altered Indian life as much as European manufactures did.

_____ 6. The colonists tacitly encouraged small-scale genocide by providing weapons to help one tribe exterminate another.

_____ 7. French kings could not get French settlers to move to Canada and did not have the power to force any to move there.

_____ 8. Intensive agriculture required exclusive use of the land, and the very concept of owning the earth was foreign to the Indians.

_____ 9. The ornate Roman Catholic ritual—the mystery of the Mass and the vivid statues—had no appeal to the Indian, the Man of Nature.

_____ 10. The word "indenture" came from the quality of paper used to write a contract, paper that was durable for a long period of time.

II. Multiple Choice

_____ 1. In 1620 when the first English ship-master at Gambia was offered slaves in payment for goods he replied

    a. we only want females for breeding

    b. we do not deal in such commodities

    c. it is illegal in England

    d. since the Bible supports it, we will accept

_____ 2. The most famous runaway indentured servant, who, in 1723 at the age of seventeen, walked out on his brother and traveled from Boston to Philadelphia, was

    a. George Washington

    b. Paul Revere

    c. Benjamin Franklin

    d. David Rittenhouse

_____ 3. As a result of their victory in the War of the Spanish Succession in 1713, the British won the right to supply Spanish America with

    a. food and textiles

    b. rum

    c. manufactured goods

    d. slaves

_____ 4. A slave who cost £5–10 in Africa in 1700 sold in the New World for

    a. £25

    b. £15

    c. £60

    d. £75

_____ 5. One thing that made it easy for outsiders to manipulate the superior numbers of Africans was

    a. fear of the white skins of white men

    b. most captured for slavery were women and children

    c. ancestral hatreds among tribes

    d. their pacifist outlook

_____ 6. Those black captives who were ill, injured, or exhausted on the march to the coast were

    a. allowed to lie in the mangrove swamp

    b. killed on the spot

    c. carried by other slaves

    d. tied and brought in later

_____ 7. The most desirable blacks to have from a village in the slave trade were

    a. women over twenty

    b. middle-aged men and women

    c. men and teenage girls

    d. children under twelve

_____ 8. The "three sisters" of the Indian diet, planted together in mounds were

    a. tomatoes, potatoes, corn

    b. corn, beans, squash

    c. pumpkins, grapes, carrots

    d. lettuce, peas, turnips

III. Quantification

Fill in each blank in the following statements with the correct number or numbers. Then determine whether you consider the statement to be very important (VI) or less important (LI). Write your choice in the blank to the left of each statement.

VI–LI

_____ 1. About _____ Indians lived in all the parts of the continent the English settled during the first century.

_____ 2. The Indians of the Americas spoke about _____ mutually unintelligible languages.

_____ 3. A typical summer village of the Powhaten in Virginia consisted of about _____ people.

_____ 4. In 1721, Pennsylvania paid $ _____ for an Algonkian warrior's scalp and $ _____ for a live prisoner.

_____ 5. The most common term for the indentured servant was _____ years.

_____ 6. By the time of the Revolution, there were about _____ slaves in the thirteen colonies, all but _____ in the South.

_____ 7. If one slave in _____ died, the profits were still considerable for the middle passage across the Atlantic.

_____ 8. A slave that cost 5–10 pounds sterling in Africa in 1700 sold in the New World for _____ pounds sterling.

_____ 9. In 1708 there were _____ Indians and 2,000 blacks in bondage in North Carolina.

IV. Concepts–Ideas

Identify each of the following key words briefly and explain the relationship between them and the words that follow in parentheses. Then in the blank to the left indicate whether you think the concept has contemporary significance (CS) or is only significant in the past (PS). For those you have marked "CS" explain the contemporary connections, that is, in what way is the concept similar to events, ideas, and developments in modern times.

CS–PS

_____ 1. fetish (supernatural — manitou — stone — bid — magicians)

_____

_____

_____ 2. diversity of Indian culture (linguistic — fragmentation — sign language — social relationships — "the people"— "other things" — physical types)

_____

_____

_____ 3. slash and burn (bark — sunlight — women — foliage — corn, beans, squash — gather, hunt)

_____

_____

_____ 4. ecological system (furs — deer — beaver — felt — extermination — short-term gain)

_____

_____

_____ 5. "counting coup" (adoption — resources — weapons — scalping — ritual demonstration — no slaughter — enmity)

_____

_____

_____ 6. owning the earth (cultivation — favor Indian culture — agriculture — air, clouds, sea — chop trees)

_____

_____

_____ 7. *coureurs de bois* (boldness — savagery — dress — forts — going native — trapping — Algonkians)

_____

_____

_____ 8. ornate ritual (universal — traditions — ceremonies — status — aesthetic — mystery)

_____

_____

_____ 9. *durante vita* (for life — dozen — servants — 1650 — tragedy — different from us)

_____

_____

_____ 10. indenture (apprenticeship — notch — price of passage — labor — not free — passage — sustenance — seven)

_____

_____

_____ 11. *Asiento de negros* (exclusive — richer than territory — sordid — mercantilism — 1713 — promiscuously)

_____

_____

_____ 12. *tumberios* (one in five — Portuguese humane — coffins — "middle passage" — "herrings in a barrel" — profit)

_____

_____

_____ 13. ancestral hatreds (farmers — maternal — weapons — divisions — language — tribe equals status)

_____

_____

_____ 14. Catholic (Church as body — Protestants — for few — everyone — Indians unacceptable — similarities)

_____

_____

V. Essay Questions

Write notes under each of the following questions that would help you answer similar essay questions on an exam.

1. Describe, in some detail, the Indian culture and style of life in North America. Include government, family life, religion, language, and culture. Do the Indians deserve the designation "uncivilized savages?" Why or why not? What do you think the word "civilized" means?

_____

_____

_____

2. Explain the Indian economy and its ecological aspects. Were the Indians better for the ecology than white hunters and farmers? Why?

_____

_____

_____

3. List and explain briefly the elements of the impact of the European on Indian life and culture. In what ways was this beneficial? In what ways harmful?

_____

_____

_____

4. Why did the French get along with the Indians better than the English and Dutch did? How does religion indicate this difference in acceptability of the French over the English?

_____

_____

_____

5. If the French were so successful with the major Indian tribes, why do you suppose they eventually lost control of North America to the English?

_____

_____

_____

6. Describe the beginnings of slavery in North America. In what ways was this a great historical tragedy?

_____

_____

_____

7. What is an indentured servant? How did the system evolve and what were the problems with the indentured servant system? Overall was it a beneficial system or an oppressive institution comparable to slavery? Explain.

_____

_____

_____

8. Describe the slave trade in detail. Should those who engaged in it be condemned or should we just conclude that they were part of the context of the times? Explain.

_____

_____

_____

9. Write an essay on the West African roots of the slaves. Would the future of West Africa have been different had so many millions of young people not been removed?

_____

_____

_____

10. Describe the process of becoming a slave. React to the New England slave trader, a pious, morally-strict Calvinist, or Quakers engaged in the trade. Can you imagine any moral justification they might advance in their defense? Explain.

_____

_____

_____

VI. Fact–Judgment

Determine whether you consider each of the following statements to be a fact (F) or a judgment (J). A judgment may be true and you may agree with it, but it remains a judgment because it is *derived from* fact and not a fact itself. It could be either a reasoned judgment or a professional interpretation. Write your choice in the blank to the left of the statement.

F–J

_____ 1. The variety of social relationships among the Indians was more diverse than it was in seventeenth century Europe.

_____ 2. Some Indians were gentle pacifists who survived only because they lived in isolated or undesirable places.

_____ 3. In North Carolina several small tribes living within 10 miles of one another for at least a century could not communicate except by sign language.

_____ 4. While there were fifty languages in North America there were only three significant linguistic groups.

_____ 5. Only with the introduction of European tools that resulted in an increased food supply were larger more permanent Indian communities established.

_____ 6. The colonists tacitly encouraged small-scale genocide among the Indians by providing the weapons that made it possible.

_____ 7. When a governor of Virginia reached the crest of the Appalachians, he celebrated by setting a table with pressed linen, fine china, and silver.

_____ 8. Not only were the French not a numerical threat to the Indians, but their economic interests seemed to favor the native peoples.

_____ 9. When the College of William and Mary was established in Virginia in 1693, provision was made for Indian education, but none showed up.

_____ 10. By the mid-1500s, before the English had any settlements, blacks were the backbone of the labor force in the West Indies and Brazil.

_____ 11. North America's greatest historical tragedy was the enslavement of millions of Africans on the basis of their race.

_____ 12. The records of masters of indentured servants complaining about stolen food and drink, rowdy parties, and pregnancies among the women are abundant.

_____ 13. Since Islam and Christianity were the faiths of the slave traders, they did not make much headway in Africa.

_____ 14. In the Ashanti tribe, descent was traced in the maternal line, and women were accorded high status.

_____ 15. Numerous slaves on the slave ship simply cracked, killing themselves or others in fits of insanity.

ANSWERS

I. True–False	II. Multiple Choice	III. Quantification	IV. Concepts–Ideas	VIII. Fact–Judgment
1. True	1. b	VI 1. 150,000	1. CS	1. J
2. False	2. c	VI 2. 500	2. CS	2. F
3. True	3. d	LI 3. 500	3. PS	3. F
4. False	4. a	VI 4. 140.00; 30.00	4. CS	4. F
5. True	5. c	LI 5. 7	5. PS	5. J
6. True	6. b	VI 6. 500,000; 50,000	6. CS	6. J
7. False	7. c	LI 7. 5	7. PS	7. F
8. True	8. b	LI 8. 25	8. CS	8. J
9. False		LI 9. 1,400	9. PS	9. F
10. False			10. PS	10. F
			11. PS	11. J
			12. PS	12. F
			13. CS	13. J
			14. CS	14. F
				15. F

6

British America in Bloom

The Colonies in the Eighteenth Century

"Leisure is the time for doing something useful."

"Time is money."

Benjamin Franklin

"Human history is in essence a history of ideas.

H. G. Wells

I. **True–False**
   If the statement is false, change any words necessary to make it true.

_____ 1.   In colonial America children grew up working and were economic assets.

_____ 2.   Benjamin Franklin was indifferent regarding slavery.

_____ 3.   Life expectancy in North America was greater than in any other continent.

_____ 4.   It was suggested in 1776 in Pennsylvania that German, not English, be the official language of the state.

_____ 5.   When faced with the prospect of losing political power in Pennsylvania, the Quakers modified their pacifist position.

_____ 6.   Colonists, showing their disdain for European affairs, called the war of 1689 the War of the League of Augsburg.

_____ 7.   Both Port Royal in 1697 and Louisbourg in 1748 were returned to France after having been captured by colonists.

_____ 8.   Only wealthy Englishmen would come to the colonies as British officials, because here they had to contend with the local assemblies for salaries and office expenses.

_____ 9.   Jonathan Edwards inspired many "false conversions" by staring at the audience during his sermons.

_____ 10. Enlightenment philosophers believed that the universe could be understood without divine revelation and that society could be improved, even perfected.

II. Multiple Choice

_____ 1. William Byrd of Virginia was

    a. not formally educated

    b. educated in Holland and England

    c. a student at William and Mary

    d. tutored until he was 21

_____ 2. General Edward Braddock

    a. was arrogant, subborn, and unimaginative

    b. engaged in germ warfare against the Indians

    c. was defeated by the French in western Pennsylvania

    d. all of the above

_____ 3. Which of the following was *not* a belief of the Enlightenment?

    a. the secrets of the universe could be unlocked by reason

    b. architecture was translated into strict laws of proportion

    c. God intervenes in nature only as an answer to prayer

    d. human society can be improved, even perfected

_____ 4. Which of the following is true about colonial politics?

    a. governors enjoyed the power of defiance of colonial assemblies by using the veto

    b. in England taxation had come to be the King's prerogative

    c. for the most part royal governors were men on the make, not the wealthy

    d. since the colonial governor's pay came from Parliament he could not be coerced by the colonial legislatures

_____ 5. The Seven Years' War in Europe was the same as which war in the colonies?

    a. French and Indian War

    b. King William's War

    c. Queen Anne's War

    d. King George's War

_____ 6. After which war did the English expel thousands of French from Acadia?

    a. Queen Anne's War

    b. War of Jenkin's Ear

    c. American Revolution

    d. King Philip's War

_____ 7. The law that required that a property owner's estate in land be bequeathed as a whole to the eldest son was known as

    a. elitism

    b. primogeniture

    c. entail

    d. inheritance

III. Quantification

Fill in each blank in the following statements with the correct number of numbers. Then determine whether you consider the statement to be very important (VI) or less important (LI). Write your choice in the blank to the left of each statement.

VI–LI

_____ 1. Benjamin Franklin went to work in his father's business full time at the age of _____ .

_____ 2. From 1700 to 1776 the population of the colonies increased from about 350,000 people to about _____ million.

_____ 3. In one period after 1700, about _____ Scotch-Irish a year emigrated to the colonies.

_____ 4. By the end of the colonial period there were about _____ blacks to every _____ whites in South Carolina.

_____ 5. George Whitefield often preached for _____ hours a week.

_____ 6. At the beginning of the French and Indian War there were about _____ French in North America compared to _____ million English in the thirteen colonies.

IV. Concepts–Ideas

Identify each of the following key words briefly and explain the relationship between them and the words that follow in parentheses.

1. bourgeois virtues (thrift — hard work — "time is money")

_____

_____

2. pacifist ideals (Quakers — peace — fair dealing — Indian land — Scotch-Irish)

_____

_____

3. field hands (West Africa — male — West Indies — sugar)

_____

_____

4. diversified economy (agriculture — candles — craftsmen)

_____

_____

5. eighteenth century warfare (rulers — diplomacy — territory — professionals — no ideology)

_____

_____

6. *la petite guerre* (harassment — warning — Indian-style)

_____

_____

7. deportations (Nova Scotia — expulsion — Louisiana — Cajuns)

_____

_____

8. salutary neglect (healthful — not disturb — forget laws — bribery — smuggling)

_____

_____

9. autonomy (erosion — prerogatives — taxation — get along)

_____

_____

10. revival (sinfulness — emotional — trauma — happiness — hereafter — release)

_____

_____

11. reason (secrets of universe — mathematical equations — "classical" — the clock of nature)

_____

_____

12. daring gambit (strike at the source — Plains of Abraham — no retreat — redrawn map)

_____

_____

13. hospitality (banquet — travelers — gentleman — manager — company — dance)

_____

_____

V. Essay Questions
Write notes under each of the following questions that would help you answer similar essay questions on an exam.

1. Compare and contrast the features of the Great Awakening with those of the Enlightenment. Which viewpoint is dominant in the United States at present?

_____

_____

2. Explain the colonial influence on and involvement in the four wars between 1689 and 1763. Were the colonists important to English success? Explain.

_____

_____

3. Describe the features of salutary neglect and political autonomy and speculate as to how they caused difficulty between Great Britain and the colonies later.

_____

_____

4. Which of the following people had the most influence on the development of eventual antagonisms between Great Britain and the colonies: Horace Walpole, George Whitefield, James Wolfe, William Pitt, or William of Orange? Choose one and defend your choice.

_____

_____

5. Compare the lifestyle of William Byrd with that of a religious Puritan.

_____

_____

6. What were the main features of eighteenth century warfare? Was it more humane than modern warfare? Explain.

_____

_____

7. What were the major decisions and events in the struggle for the North American continent? Explain each briefly.

_____

_____

8. Describe the struggles between the Scotch-Irish and the Quakers. Should the Quakers have retired from political involvement because of their clash with the Scotch-Irish? Why?

_____

_____

9. In what ways had the colonies become much more independent through the period from 1700 to 1763? Be specific. Do you think this growing independence was noticeable at the time? Why?

_____

_____

10. Write an essay on the life of William Byrd. Would you consider him a great or important man? Why or why not?

_____

_____

_____

VI Fact–Judgment–Importance

Determine whether you consider each of the following statements to be a fact (F) or a judgment (J). A judgment may be true and you may agree with it, but it remains a judgment because it is *derived from* fact and not a fact itself. It could be either a reasoned judgment or a professional interpretation. Also decide whether each statement is very important (VI) or less important (LI). Write your choices in the blanks to the left of the statement.

F–J   VI–LI

_____ _____ 1. Benjamin Franklin was never behind on a trend, and capitalized on every opportunity provided in a changing America.

_____ _____ 2. Franklin supported an aggressive foreign policy, and in Europe lobbied on behalf of American interests.

_____ _____ 3. After 1700, migrants from Europe and Africa crossed the Atlantic in numbers never dreamed of before that time.

_____ _____ 4. The Scotch-Irish were a combative people, and they did not mellow in American air.

_____ _____ 5. The American population became less English in the eighteenth century.

_____ _____ 6. The people of the British Isles include not only the English and the Scots, but also the Welsh and the Irish.

_____ _____ 7. The total colonial population of 2.8 million was greater than the populations of several European countries.

_____ _____ 8. From 1689 to 1763 the colonists participated in a series of wars that won for them a luxurious security unknown to Europeans.

_____ _____ 9. In taking over Acadia (Novia Scotia) the English were responsible for one of the first tragic deportations in American history.

_____ _____ 10. Under prime minister Robert Walpole the Navigation Acts were largely ignored because of salutary neglect, bribery, and open defiance.

_____ _____ 11. In the atmosphere of toleration one of the peculiarities of American life took root—the bewildering multiplicity of religious denominations.

_____ _____ 12. Revivals aimed at stimulating the trauma of salvation, and this catharsis offered a release from the difficulties of life.

_____ _____ 13. Braddock's reputation now is even lower than it was at the time he engaged in what was in effect, germ warfare, by seeing to it that smallpox-infected blankets fell into the hands of the Indians.

F–J   VI–LI

_____ _____ 14. So as not to break up an estate, "second sons" in a wealthy family might serve in the military or be educated to the ministry or to another profession.

_____ _____ 15. George Washington indicated that he was well imbued with getting ahead and moving up in the world when he proposed to a propertied widow, Martha Curtis.

_____ _____ 16. In most colonies, husbands were not permitted to beat their wives, a restriction largely unknown in the old world.

ANSWERS

I. True–False	II. Multiple Choice	III. Quantification	VI. Fact–Judgment–Importance
1. True	1. b	LI 1. 10	1. J LI
2. False	2. d	VI 2. 8	2. J VI
3. True	3. c	LI 3. 4,000	3. J VI
4. True	4. c	VI 4. 5; 7	4. J LI
5. False	5. a	LI 5. 40	5. J VI
6. False	6. a	VI 6. 50,000; 1.2	6. F VI
7. True	7. b		7. F VI
8. False			8. J VI
9. False			9. J V I
10. True			10. J VI
			11. J VI
			12. J LI
			13. J LI
			14. F VI
			15. J LI
			16. F VI

⊰═7═⊱

Years of Tumult

The Quarrel with the Mother Country, 1763–1770

"We do strictly forbid, on pain of our displeasure, all our loving subjects from making any purchases or settlements whatever, west of the line."

"Historians relate, not so much what is done, as what they would have believed."

Benjamin Franklin

I. True–False
If the statement is false, change any words necessary to make it true.

_____ 1. As a result of the mixing of cultures, one tendency of the Iroquois was to abandon the single-family log cabin and to live by class in long houses.

_____ 2. The British finally convinced the French Canadians to abandon their French language and learn English.

_____ 3. Actual protest over the Proclamation of 1763 was minimal, yet later colonists came to view it as an example of British interference with their way of life.

_____ 4. British administration was corrupt and top-heavy with officials who lived off public funds.

_____ 5. The act of 1764 taxed British and foreign molasses equally, which meant its purpose was to control trade and not raise revenue.

_____ 6. All money raised from the Stamp Act of 1765 was to be used in defending, protecting, and securing the colonies.

_____ 7. The Stamp Act Congress delegates refused to acknowledge their subordination to the King.

_____ 8. Washington and other Virginians were elected to the House of Burgesses from counties where they did not reside.

_____ 9. George II preferred to speak French over English and took no interest in government.

_____ 10. Descent among the Iroquois was traced through the maternal line.

II. Multiple Choice

_____ 1. Which of the following was not a *result* of the Proclamation Act of 1763?

    a. Pontiac's Rebellion
    b. Americans viewed it as interference with expansion
    c. there was a freeze on the sale of land in the western regions
    d. the imaginary line was not considered permanent

_____ 2. One item taxed in the Townshend Duties that could not be produced in the colonies was

    a. paint
    b. glass
    c. tea
    d. lead

_____ 3. Imports from England in the period from 1740 to 1770

    a. decreased
    b. more than doubled
    c. remained about the same
    d. about equalled exports to England

_____ 4. The Stamp Act of 1765 taxed all but which of the following:

    a. postage in the colonies
    b. legal documents
    c. newspapers
    d. playing cards

_____ 5. James Otis suggested in a speech before the Stamp Act Congress in 1765 that

    a. Americans were already represented in Parliament
    b. the colonists should be allowed to elect members to Parliament
    c. virtual representation was true representation
    d. members of Parliament represent the colonies also

_____ 6. The Declaratory Act stated that

    a. taxation of the colonists without their consent was to end
    b. there would be no more Stamp taxes
    c. external taxes would replace internal taxes
    d. Parliament had the right and power to make laws for the colonies in all cases

_____ 7. Unquestionably, as a symbol that unified the British people, everyone agreed on the importance of the

    a. rights of Englishmen
    b. idea of no taxation without representation
    c. monarch
    d. British navy

III. Quantification

Fill in each blank in the following statements with the correct number or numbers. Then determine whether you consider the statement to be very important (VI) or less important (LI). Also decide whether the statement is simple and complete in itself (SC) or whether it is open to many interpretations (MI) and needs more data to give it meaning. Write your choices in the blanks to the left of each statement.

VI–LI   SC–MI

_____   _____   1.   Expense of maintaining British soldiers (permanent garrison of 10,000 men in America) was $ _____ a year.

_____   _____   2.   The cost of governing the colonies in 1764 was £ _____ a year while the colonial trade brought at least £ _____ million into Great Britain.

_____   _____   3.   English landowners paid _____ percent of the value of their property in taxes each year.

_____   _____   4.   Grenville calculated (perhaps inaccurately) that average English taxpayers paid an annual tax of _____ shillings while a British subject in Massachusetts paid _____ shilling a year and the average Virginian only _____ pence.

_____   _____   5.   In 1766, the molasses duty was reduced to a _____ a barrel, the level of the traditional bribe.

_____   _____   6.   In October 1765, _____ delegates from _____ colonies assembled in New York City as the Stamp Act Congress.

_____   _____   7.   The Townshend Act duties were supposed to bring in _____ pounds sterling annually, but they actually yielded _____ in 1768 and _____ in 1769.

IV. Concepts–Ideas

Identify each of the following key words briefly and explain the relationship between them and the words that follow in parentheses.

1.   centrally administered (self-support — new policy — King-in-Parliament — London officials — one set of rules)

_____

_____

2.   local juries (acquittal — friends — bribes — vice-admiralty courts)

_____

_____

3.   "parliaments" (elected assemblies — thirteen — representation — taxation)

_____

_____

4. constitutional distinction (internal direct tax — control of trade — external trade — John Dickinson)

_____

_____

5. use of violence (roughing up — burning — looting — threats)

_____

_____

6. virtual representation (represent the nation — Washington's election county — small proportion vote)

_____

_____

7. shifting factions (little cliques — half a dozen — alliances of convenience — graft — public office)

_____

_____

8. "be a King" (King's friends — patronage — erratic — stubborn — mediocrities— inconsistent)

_____

_____

9. boycott (merchants — petitions for repeal — imports or external tax — Declaratory Act)

_____

_____

10. technological impact (guns — metal tools — logs — single-family cabins — corn)

_____

_____

V. Essay Questions

Write notes under each of the following questions that would help you answer similar essay questions on an exam.

1. Compare the Iroquois style of life with that of the white settler. Were the Indians and settlers just two different cultures or was one more civilized than the other? Explain.

_____

_____

_____

2. Explain the differences in the views of representation held by the British and the Americans and point out which you feel to be better for the strength of a nation.

_____

_____

3. List and explain briefly the major British government acts regarding the thirteen colonies from 1763 to 1770 and then choose which one you believe to be the most significant. Defend your choice.

_____

_____

4. Argue the British side in the debate over the colonies especially regarding taxation, representation, and costs of empire. Was the British side more "in the right" than the American side? Explain.

_____

_____

5. Imagine that you are Prime Minister in Parliament in the 1760s. How would you have acquired revenue from the colonies without provoking protest and boycott? Use your imagination.

_____

_____

6. Argue the proposition that the differences between the British government and colonists were primarily a struggle for political power rather than a debate over economic issues. Be specific in your examples or evidence.

_____

_____

7. How would 20 American representatives sitting in Parliament have changed the course of events in the 1760s (if at all)?

_____

_____

8. Would you conclude that a revolution for independence of the thirteen colonies was inevitable by 1770? Give evidence to support your viewpoint.

_____

_____

_____

9. Describe the Townshend Duties. Were they fair? Why or why not?

_____

_____

_____

10. Evaluate the leadership of George III. Was he a tyrant or merely incompetent? To what extent was the Revolution his fault? Explain.

_____

_____

_____

11. Write an essay on the Stamp Act episode in American history. Include the American reaction to it. Should the British have been suitably warned by the American reaction to this Act? Explain.

_____

_____

_____

VI. Ranking

Rank each of the following decisions from 1 to 10 according to your assessment of their importance in bringing about the conflict of the American Revolution. The most important would be 1, and the least important would be 10.

1–10

_____ a. Decision by Sir Jeffrey Amherst in 1763 not to continue the French practice of presenting gifts of European goods to the Indians.

_____ b. Privy Council in 1763 drew an imaginary line on the Appalachian Divide and forbade settlement or purchases of land west of the line.

_____ c. Parliament's passage of the Quartering Act of 1765 charging the cost of British troops' shelter, food, and drink to the colony in which they were posted.

_____ d. Greenville's decision to tax both British and foreign molasses equally and to name the act the American Revenue Act.

_____ e. The Grenville decision to include in the Sugar Act a stipulation that customs service cases would be tried in vice-admiralty courts with no jury.

_____ f. Decision to pass the Stamp Act and apply it not only to legal documents (as in England) but to newspapers, pamphlets, playing cards, and handbills.

_____ g. Decision of nine colonies to send 37 delegates to New York City to protest the Stamp Act.

_____ h. Decision by George III to "be a King" and to organize his own parliamentary faction, the "King's friends."

_____ i. The decision by merchants to organize a boycott of British goods in reaction to the Townshend Duties.

_____ j. Decision by the Iroquois to shun Christian missionaries and to reject the white settlers' way of life.

1. For the two decisions that you gave the highest rank, explain why you consider them the most important.

   a. _____

   _____

   _____

   b. _____

   _____

   _____

2. For the decision that you gave the lowest rank, explain why you consider it the least important.

   _____

   _____

   _____

VII. Fact–Judgment

Determine whether you consider each of the following statements to be a fact (F) or a judgment (J). A judgment may be true and you may agree with it, but it remains a judgment because it is *derived from* fact and not a fact itself. It could be either a reasoned judgment or a professional interpretation. Write your choice in the blank to the left of the statement.

F–J

_____ 1. British colonial policy was never tyrannical.

_____ 2. Between 1763 and 1773 trans-Appalachian lands were opened to speculation and settlement.

_____ 3. British administration was corrupt and top-heavy with officials who lived off public funds without doing anything in particular.

_____ 4. Americans did not want to pay taxes and much of their protest over the Sugar Act of 1764 was an expression of sheer self-interest.

_____ 5. The right to trial by jury was, in their own eyes, what set the English and the colonists apart from other nationalities.

_____ 6. Richard Henry Lee, who would later introduce the resolution for independence in 1776, applied for a job as a stamp collector in 1765.

_____ 7. The actions of the British government were limited by a mixed collection of historic documents and customs that had not been written down but were binding nevertheless.

_____ 8. The Americans took their "rights as British subjects," as they stubbornly interpreted them, quite seriously.

_____ 9. The wording of the Declaratory Act, which stated that Parliament had the power to make laws for Americans, was lifted from a law of 1719 that had made Ireland completely subject to Great Britain.

_____ 10. As Prime Minister, Lord Chatham had been a good friend to America, but his taking ill in 1766 was an accident that changed the course of events when it forced him to drop out of government.

_____ 11. George III was not an evil man and not a tyrant, but he was erratic, vain, stubborn, and not especially intelligent.

_____ 12. During the boycott of the Townshend Duties, English merchants flooded Parliament with petitions for repeal of the duties.

ANSWERS

I. True–False	II. Multiple Choice	III. Quantification			VII. Fact–Judgment
1. True	1. a	VI	MI	1. 200,000	1. J
2. False	2. c	VI	MI	2. 350,000; 2	2. F
3. True	3. b	VI	SC	3. 20	3. J
4. True	4. a	VI	MI	4. 26; 1; 5	4. J
5. True	5. b	LI	MI	5. penny	5. J
6. True	6. d	VI	MI	6. 37; 9	6. F
7. False	7. c	VI	MI	7. 40,000; 13,000; 3,000	7. F
8. True					8. J
9. True					9. F
10. True					10. J–F
					11. J
					12. F

⊹⊱8⊰⊹

From Riot to Rebellion

The Road to Independence, 1770–1776

"In the name of the great Jehovah and the Continental Congress."

"It is a mark of civilized man that he seeks to understand his traditions, and to criticize them, not to swallow them whole."

M. I. Finley

I. True–False
If the statement is false, change any words necessary to make it true.

_____ 1. Benjamin Franklin persuaded the Paxton Boys to withdraw by promising a more humane Indian policy.

_____ 2. John Adams was proud of the Boston crowds and defended their behavior in court.

_____ 3. Patrick Henry denounced George III because the king reversed a law that had been passed by the Virginia House of Burgesses.

_____ 4. Few of the 55 men who gathered for the first Continental Congress had ever met.

_____ 5. On the same day as the Battle of Lexington, Parliament banned Massachusetts fishermen from the Grand Banks of Newfoundland.

_____ 6. Thomas Paine favored an American Parliament with the retention of our loyalty to King George III.

_____ 7. Congress altered the Declaration of Independence by deleting the attack on the institution of slavery.

_____ 8. The first shot at Lexington was fired by Major Pitcairn of the British army.

_____ 9. After the battle of Bunker Hill, General Clinton concluded that such victories would destroy the British ability to fight.

_____ 10. Thomas Jefferson did not try to be original in writing the Declaration of Independence.

II. Multiple Choice

_____ 1. The "writs of assistance" were
   a. laws requiring colonial help in British wars
   b. another name for stamps under the Stamp Act
   c. general search warrants to allow a search for smuggled goods
   d. James Otis' prosecution techniques

_____ 2. The Quebec Act of 1774 provided for all but which of the following?
   a. recognition of the French language for Quebec
   b. restricted Quebec to the St. Lawrence River area
   c. recognized the Catholic religion for the French in Quebec
   d. provided for no elective assembly for French Canadians

_____ 3. The resolution for independence was solidly supported by
   a. New England
   b. the Middle Colonies
   c. John Dickinson
   d. New York

_____ 4. In the battle of Bunker Hill (Breed's Hill), which is true?
   a. Americans charged the British head-on
   b. the British suffered 5,000 casualties
   c. the British could not take the hill
   d. Americans yielded the hill in the face of British bayonets

III. Quantification

Fill in each blank in the following statements with the correct number or numbers. Then determine whether you consider the statement to be very important (VI) or less important (LI). Write your choice in the blank to the left of each statement.

VI–LI

_____ 1. Samuel Adams distributed _____ of woodcut prints showing aggressive soldiers, in the Boston Massacre, shooting innocent Bostonians.

_____ 2. The governor of New York dissolved the Assembly in 1766 when its members refused to provide the redcoats _____ pints of beer or _____ ounces of rum a day.

_____ 3. The Americans at Lexington were outnumbered _____ to _____ .

_____ 4. When the British finally got back to Boston after the Lexington and Concord battles, _____ of their expedition were dead or wounded.

_____ 5. Within a few years, a country with a population of _____ million bought _____ copies of Thomas Paine's Common Sense.

_____ 6. The British took Bunker Hill (actually Breed's Hill) at a cost of _____ casualties.

IV. Concepts –Ideas

Identify each of the following key words briefly and explain the relationship between them and the words that follow in parentheses.

1. writs of assistance (search warrant — smuggle — enter property)

_____

_____

2. the "crowd" (poor — nothing to lose — seamen — outcasts — boldness)

_____

_____

3. tavern social life (social hall — tea, rum — "the ordinary" — British soldiers)

_____

_____

4. Redcoats (resented — tax to support — dregs of society — punished — no rights — clique)

_____

_____

5. sectionalism (Paxton Boys — Regulators — county governments — aggressive Indian policy)

_____

_____

6. monopoly (East India Company — bankruptcy — surplus — undersell — precedent)

_____

_____

7. coercion (punish — closed port — trials — Redcoats in homes — Quebec)

_____

_____

8. "gentlemen" (never met — merchants, planters, professionals — lavish meals — in common)

_____

_____

9. warfare (artillery — fife and drum — muskets — drills — not flee)

_____

_____

10. independence (thread of sentiment — "free and independent states" — Pennsylvania — July 2)

_____

_____

11. declaration (Jefferson's two weeks — propaganda — King George — grievances — human rights)

_____

_____

12. black equality (Banneker — almanac — letter to Jefferson — pacifist Quaker — inventions)

_____

_____

V. Essay Questions

Write notes under each of the following questions that would help you answer similar essay questions on an exam.

1. What steps led to the American Revolution from 1770 to 1776?

_____

_____

_____

2. Point out the differences between the first and second Continental Congresses.

_____

_____

_____

3. Explain whether you think propaganda and emotion were more or were less important than hard economic factors in bringing on the American Revolution. Give evidence to support your viewpoint.

_____

_____

_____

4. Take the British side in the events and developments from 1770 to 1776. What evidence would you present to support a view that the British were reasonable and just?

_____

_____

_____

5. Which battle was most important in the coming of the American Revolution—Lexington, Bunker Hill, or Fort Ticonderoga? Explain why.

_____

_____

_____

6. Explain the ideas of Thomas Paine in *Common Sense*. Do they "make sense"? Why or why not?

_____

_____

_____

7. Write an essay about the two blacks, Phyllis Wheatley and Benjamin Banneker, and their accomplishments.

_____

_____

_____

8. Describe the dangerous relationship between British troops and street people. Do you believe this antagonism is exaggerated or was it a real factor in the coming of the Revolution? Explain.

_____

_____

_____

9. What were the contributions of James Otis and Patrick Henry to the American Revolution?

_____

_____

_____

10. Explain the Intolerable Acts. Did Boston deserve this treatment? Why or why not?

_____

_____

_____

VI. Ranking

Rank the following ten events that led to the American Revolution from 1 to 10 according to their influence on the decision to revolt against England. The most important would be 1, and the least important would be 10.

1–10

_____ a. Boston Massacre

_____ b. *Gaspée* Incident

_____ c. Patrick Henry's speech

_____ d. Tea Act

_____ e. Intolerable Acts

_____ f. Suffolk Resolves

_____ g. battle at Lexington

_____ h. battle at Fort Ticonderoga

_____ i. publication of *Common Sense*

_____ j. adoption of the Declaration of Independence

1. For the two events that you gave the highest ranking, explain why you consider them the most important.

a. _____

_____

_____

b. _____

_____

_____

VII. Chronology

Number the following twelve events in their correct chronological order from 1 to 12.

1–12

_____ a. burning of the *Gaspée*

_____ b. Boston Tea Party

_____ c. Battle of Ticonderoga

_____ d. adoption of the Declaration of Independence

_____ e. meeting of the First Continental Congress

_____ f. Boston Massacre

_____ g. Paxton Boys march on Philadelphia

_____ h. Intolerable (Coercive Acts) against Boston

_____ i. Patrick Henry's denunciation of George III

_____ j. Battle of Lexington

_____ k. publication of *Common Sense*

_____ l. Sam Adams' speech on natural rights

VIII. Determining Importance

Determine whether you consider the following statements to be very important (VI) or less important (LI). Write your choice in the blank to the left of each statement.

VI–LI

_____ 1. The British may have missed an opportunity to retain the colonies when they failed to exploit the hostility between western farmers and eastern elites.

_____ 2. John Adams was defense attorney for the soldiers involved in the Boston Massacre and argued that the mob was to blame.

_____ 3. Several soldiers involved in the Boston Massacre were branded on the hand.

_____ 4. Wealthy taxpayers resented paying the expenses of British soldiers and ordinary working people disliked rubbing shoulders with them.

_____ 5. Colonial crowds were made up overwhelmingly of poor or marginally employed young men, who had little to lose as a consequence of rash actions.

_____ 6. The East India Company handled many governmental functions in the eastern part of the British Empire.

_____ 7. The participants in the Boston Tea Party returned the next morning to destroy the chests of tea still floating.

_____ 8. Contrary to Lord North's expectations, the Coercive Acts against Massachusetts angered important groups in every colony so much that twelve of them sent delegates to a "continental congress."

_____ 9. The key to winning battles in the eighteenth century was long, hard, tedious training.

_____ 10. Like many English officers, Major John Pitcairn was not anxious to kill Americans at Lexington.

_____ 11. Americans fired on the British at Breed's Hill when they could "see the whites of their eyes."

_____ 12. George III refused to listen to American suggestions for peace and then backed a plan to hire German mercenaries to crush the rebellion.

IX. Fact–Judgment

Determine whether you consider each of the following statements to be a fact (F) or a judgment (J). A judgment may be true and you may agree with it, but it remains a judgment because it is *derived from* fact and not a fact itself. It could be either a reasoned judgment or a professional interpretation. Write your choice in the blank to the left of the statement.

_____ 1. In 1770 the majority of Americans wanted calm, business as usual, and a resumption of normal daily life.

_____ 2. The Red Coats in Boston had more to do with the anti-British feelings of lower-class colonials than did the tax laws.

_____ 3. King George bore the brunt of Jefferson's attack in the Declaration of Independence.

_____ 4. Every American who could read must have at least skimmed through *Common Sense*.

_____ 5. The "Declaration of the Cause and Necessity of Taking up Arms" of July 1775 denied any motive but the defense of their liberties under the British flag.

_____ 6. Nowhere was the psychological impact of the victories in the north by Ethan Allen and Benedict Arnold greater than in the Second Continental Congress in Philadelphia.

_____ 7. James Otis' contribution to the agitation of the 1760s may have had as much to do with personal political disappointments as with commitment to a principle.

_____ 8. The Sons of Liberty, who ignited the last phase of the revolutionary movement with the Boston Tea Party of 1773, assembled over a barrel of rum.

_____ 9. Many Regulators in the Carolinas fought on the British side while others pushed beyond the Appalachians so they could remain neutral.

_____ 10. Although the tea sold under the Tea Act was cheap, the monopoly to the East India Company was a precedent both dangerous and obvious.

X. Ranking

Rank the following factors from 1 to 10 according to your assessment of its importance in bringing on the American Revolution. The most important would be 1, and the least important 10.

1–10

_____ a. British soldiers stationed in eastern cities.

_____ b. The various tax bills passed by Parliament.

_____ c. The colonial view that the British were infringing on the liberties of Americans.

_____ d. The American belief that they were represented in their own colonial assemblies, not in the British Parliament.

_____ e. The existence of an unemployed, hard-drinking crowd in Boston.

_____ f. The propaganda exploits of Samuel Adams (Boston Massacre) and Thomas Jefferson (Declaration of Independence)

_____ g. British decision to hire German mercenary troops.

_____ h. The acts of a handful of defiant men (Patrick Henry, James Otis, delegates to congress, minute-men at Lexington, Thomas Paine, and Samuel Adams).

_____ i. Merchants who wanted to be free of British economic restrictions and control.

_____ j. Long distance between England and the colonies and the poor communication between the two.

1. For the two factors you gave the highest rank, explain why you consider them the most important.

a. _____

_____

_____

b. _____

_____

_____

ANSWERS

I. True–False	II. Multiple Choice	III. Quantification	VII. Chronology		VIII. Determining Importance	
1. False	1. c	VI 1. hundreds	a.	5	1.	VI
2. False	2. b	LI 2. 5; 4	b.	6	2.	LI
3. True	3. a	LI 3. 10; 1	c.	10	3.	LI
4. True	4. d	VI 4. 250	d.	11	4.	VI
5. True		VI 5. 2.5; 500,000	e.	8	5.	LI
6. False		LI 6. 1,200	f.	3	6.	LI
7. True			g.	2	7.	LI
8. False			h.	7	8.	VI
9. True			i.	1	9.	LI
10. True			j.	9	10.	VI
			k.	12	11.	LI
			l.	4	12.	VI

IX. Fact–Judgment

1	J
2.	J
3.	F
4.	J
5.	F
6.	J
7.	J
8.	F
9.	F
10.	J

9

The War for Independence

Winning the Revolution, 1776–1781

"Which is better, to be ruled by one tyrant three thousand miles away, or by three thousand tyrants not a mile away?"

Reverend Mather Byles

"These are the times that try men's souls."

Thomas Paine

"The history of the world is none other than the progress of freedom."

Hegel

I. True–False
If the statement is false, change any words necessary to make it true.

_____ 1. George Washington felt that the American militia were his most reliable troops and could be depended upon.

_____ 2. What we know for certain is that militant revolutionaries made up a majority at the beginning of the war.

_____ 3. General Howe soldiered by the book and so went into winter quarters in New York in 1776.

_____ 4. Very valuable to the American cause was an engineering specialist, Tadeusz Kosciuski.

_____ 5. There was an abundance of loyalists in New England and the coastal counties of the South.

_____ 6. Records show many incidents of patriots harassing loyalists after the war, so plenty of pro-British people stayed in America.

_____ 7. The French aristocracy deluded themselves in believing that their own peasants and the "primitive" Americans led happy, wholesome lives because they were so close to nature.

_____ 8. When Washington crossed the Delaware River into Pennsylvania, his men increased their morale and their numbers increased.

_____ 9.   George Washington was not by nature an innovator.

_____ 10. Beginning in Georgia in December 1778, the Americans won a series of victories over British regulars.

II.   Multiple Choice

_____ 1. Approximately how many Americans fought on the British side?

   a.   150,000
   b.   15,000
   c.   1,500
   d.   50,000

_____ 2. Benjamin Franklin's success as a diplomat was partially due to

   a.   his sophisticated dress and manners
   b.   his playing the part of a Quaker
   c.   his devotion to France and French culture
   d.   his use of a wig and European style

_____ 3. All but which of the following is true of George Washington:

   a.   he read many books on a wide range of subjects
   b.   he contributed no important documents to the Revolution
   c.   he lacked originality
   d.   he held the cause together by "character"

_____ 4. Washington won at Yorktown because of all of the following except

   a.   he faked a maneuver around New York to keep the British busy there
   b.   the French admiral controlled the mouth of the Chesapeake Bay
   c.   Cornwallis panicked and surrendered quickly
   d.   he outnumbered the French more than two to one

_____ 5. The Treaty of Paris provided for all but which of the following:

   a.   independence for America
   b.   Americans to fish only off their own coast
   c.   no more seizure of Loyalist property
   d.   boundary settlement between the U.S. and Canada

_____ 6. Washington's great military contribution to independence lay in his skill at

   a.   training his men
   b.   promoting accuracy of canon fire
   c.   getting men to reenlist
   d.   retreating

_____ 7. In Paris, Franklin and his fellow diplomats were waiting for news like that of

   a.   the victory at Saratoga
   b.   a British offer to compromise
   c.   Spain's entry into the war
   d.   the arrival in America of French supplies

67

III. Quantification

Fill in each blank in the following statements with the correct number or numbers. Then determine whether you consider the statement to be very important (VI) or of symbolic importance in which the actual number is not very important (SI). Write your choice in the blank to the left of each statement.

VI–SI

_____ 1. The total number of Hessians on British contract during the American Revolution was _____ .

_____ 2. By 1778 the British had _____ troops in North America, while Washington considered it a good day when he could field _____ .

_____ 3. At the end of the Revolutionary War, as many as _____ Americans (1 in 30) left their native land for England.

_____ 4. At Trenton on Christmas night, 1776, Washington captured a Hessian garrison, while suffering only _____ American casualties.

_____ 5. At the Battle of Saratoga, Burgoyne surrendered _____ soldiers to Gates.

_____ 6. The British occupied New York and still had _____ troops in North America after the Battle of Yorktown.

_____ 7. When de Grasse arrived with more troops, the Americans and French at Yorktown outnumbered Cornwallis _____ to _____ .

IV. Concepts–Ideas

Identify each of the following key words briefly and explain the relationship between them and the words that follow in parentheses.

1. Loyalists (50,000 — one third — left alone — harassment)

_____

_____

2. winter quarters (the book — convenient location — snuffed out — William Howe)

_____

_____

3. "Father of his country" (no thinker — unexciting — defeats — intangibles — "character")

_____

_____

4. wilderness of America (Saratoga — foot paths — local militia — backtrack — surrender)

_____

_____

5. "America's oldest friend" (money — men — fleet — diplomacy — informal assistance)

_____

_____

6. mercenaries (unemployed military professionals — idealistic — "twist lion's tail" —specialists)

_____

_____

7. "The World Turn'd Upside Down" (Cornwallis — 17,000 — futile defense — contempt)

_____

_____

8. retreat (Long Island — slip away — sneak — abandon — bedraggled — escape — flee — demoralized — almost annihilation — in the field)

_____

_____

V. Essay Questions

Write notes under each of the following questions that would help you answer similar essay questions on an exam.

1. In the context of the American Revolution, how would you distinguish between patriots and traitors?

_____

_____

_____

2. What was the plight of the Loyalists (Tories) in the American Revolution?

_____

_____

_____

3. In 1776 would you have bet on the Americans to succeed in the struggle for independence? Why or why not?

_____

_____

_____

4. Describe the military action which took place in 1776. What do you consider to be the most significant military event in 1776? Explain why.

_____

_____

_____

5. Was Washington an *indispensable* man for the success of the American Revolution? Why?

_____

_____

_____

6. How would the actions of Howe and Burgoyne demonstrate the mistakes and perhaps incompetence of the British in the Revolution? Be specific.

_____

_____

_____

7. List the help offered by the French in the American Revolution. Was this aid essential for American success?

_____

_____

_____

8. Describe the two battles which you consider most important in the Revolution. Explain why they were important.

_____

_____

_____

9. Describe the campaigns of 1781 and the final battle at Yorktown. Would such a chain of events been predictable in January 1781? Why or why not?

_____

_____

_____

10. Explain the reasons for the American victory over the British in the American Revolution.

_____

_____

_____

VI. Historical Judgments

Which three of the following events or decisions do you consider to be the most important turning points leading to American victory in the Revolution? Indicate the three most important by writing the numbers 1, 2, and 3 in the blank spaces to the left. Then place an "X" before those three you consider to be least important as turning points.

1–2–3–X

_____ 1. Founding of the Bank of North America as a clearing house for the finances of the Revolutionary government.

_____ 2. Writing and adoption of the Articles of Confederation.

_____ 3. Writing and adoption of state constitutions, 1776–78.

_____ 4. Diplomatic negotiations leading to the Peace of Paris, 1781–83.

_____ 5. Decision by Count François de Grasse, in September 1781, to enter the Chesapeake Bay and drive off British evacuation ships in their effort to rescue Cornwallis.

_____ 6. Decision by European military professionals to volunteer to help Americans.

_____ 7. French recognition of the United States as an independent nation and signing of a formal treaty of alliance in 1778.

_____ 8. American victory over Burgoyne at the Battle of Saratoga in 1777.

_____ 9. Washington's surprise victory over the Hessians at Trenton in December 1776.

_____ 10. Washington's decisions from August 1776 to November 1776 to continually retreat in the face of British pressure.

_____ 11. Howe's decision to go into winter quarters in December 1776.

_____ 12. French government decision to funnel money and arms to American rebels in May 1776.

In the space provided below, write a brief essay defending your three choices and explaining why other possible choices were rejected.

_____

_____

_____

_____

_____

_____

_____

_____

_____

_____

_____

VII. Significant–Interesting

For each of the following statements, determine which you think to be very important and significant (S) or merely interesting or of lesser importance (I). Write your choice in the blank space at the left of each statement.

S–I

_____ 1. When he set up headquarters in New York, Howe was received more as a liberator than as a conqueror.

_____ 2. As in all times in human history, many people wished only to be left alone to pursue their daily lives.

_____ 3. There was a considerable pro-American, anti-war sentiment in England, even among powerful members of Parliament.

_____ 4. Many of the French aristocracy believed that the "primitive" Americans led happy, wholesome lives because they were close to nature.

_____ 5. Franklin appeared at the French court wearing homespun wool clothing, no wig, and rimless bifocal spectacles.

_____ 6. Howe infuriated Washington by sounding the bugle call of the chase when the Americans retreated from New York City.

_____ 7. When Washington retreated through New Jersey, in Philadelphia Congress panicked and fled to Baltimore.

_____ 8. To explain Washington's accomplishment it is necessary to list intangibles—integrity, dignity, and aristocratic bearing.

_____ 9. On Burgoyne's march south into New York his baggage included much clothing, his mistress, linen, china, crystal, and silverware.

_____ 10. In 1778 Vergennes averted a war between Prussia and Austria that would have tied down French troops in Europe.

_____ 11. When Congress failed to pay troops during 1780 and 1781, mutinies erupted among Connecticut, Pennsylvania, and New Jersey troops.

_____ 12. Since 1763, the major powers of Europe had been uneasy with Great Britain's preeminence and should be expected to encourage any challenge to it.

ANSWERS

I. True–False	II. Multiple Choice	III. Quantification	VII. Significant–Interesting
1. False	1. d	VI 1. 30,000	1. S
2. False	2. b	VI 2. 50,000; 5,000	2. I
3. True	3. a	VI 3. 100,000	3. S
4. True	4. c	SI 4. 5	4. I
5. False	5. b	SI 5. 5	5. I
6. True	6. d	VI 6. 54,000	6. I
7. True	7. a	VI 7. 17,000; 8,000	7. I
8. False			8. S
9. True			9. I
10. False			10. S
			11. S
			12. S

⊷10⊷

Inventing a Country

American Constitutions, 1781–1789

"The people are turbulent and changing; they seldom judge or determine right."

Alexander Hamilton

"In analyzing history, do not be too profound, for often the causes are quite superficial."

Emerson

I. True–False
If the statement is false, change any words necessary to make it true.

_____ 1. The men who wrote the Constitution agreed that an excess of democracy was the chief weakness of the government under the Articles of Confederation.

_____ 2. Under the finished Constitution, the states became mere administrative units.

_____ 3. The concept of "judicial review" as a power of the Supreme Court was finally written into the Constitution after long debate.

_____ 4. The American Constitution can be amended by Congress in order to make the Supreme Court conform to its wishes.

_____ 5. A Bill of Rights was not written into state constitutions but was left for the central government to include in its constitution.

_____ 6. Congress, under the Articles of Confederation, could wage war, but individual states could also wage war with the consent of Congress.

_____ 7. Eventually Congress allowed the purchase of a quarter-quarter section of land, the classic midwestern American farm of 400 acres.

_____ 8. In most states the property qualification for voting was so low that few free white males were excluded.

_____ 9. When news arrived that New York had approved the new Constitution, Virginia quickly approved it also.

_____ 10. What was singular about the American Revolution was the necessity of inventing a country from scratch.

II. Multiple Choice

_____ 1. Among the objections to the Constitution by the anti-Federalists was that

    a. the Bill of Rights was too liberal

    b. Jefferson had not helped write it

    c. free republican institutions survived only in small countries

    d. it gave the states too much power

_____ 2. Which of the following statements regarding ratification is _not_ true:

    a. the Massachusetts vote was close

    b. North Carolina approved unanimously

    c. Rhode Island held out until May 1790

    d. the vote in Virginia was 89 to 79 in favor

_____ 3. The "Great Compromise" involved

    a. settlement of the slavery issue

    b. reduction of the states to administrative units

    c. allowing the Supreme Court "judicial review"

    d. granting each state two senators regardless of the size of the state

_____ 4. The new state constitutions of 1776–78 provided for

    a. strong governors

    b. establishment of the Episcopal Church

    c. ratification by popular elections

    d. terms of six years for the legislature

_____ 5. Washington feared that disorders like Shay's rebellion were the natural consequence of

    a. French influence

    b. excessive democracy

    c. Thomas Paine's writings

    d. soldiers returning home with guns

_____ 6. According to Hamilton, "All communities divide themselves into

    a. the few and the many"

    b. revolutionaries and conservatives"

    c. Republicans and Democrats"

    d. the governors and the governed"

_____ 7. Federalists argued in _The Federalist Papers_ that a powerful United States would guarantee

    a. supremacy on the continent

    b. the safety of Europe

    c. a healthy economy

    d. liberty

III. Quantification

Fill in the blanks in the following statements with the correct number or numbers. Then in the space to the left of each statement place the numbers 1, 2, and 3 before those three items which you consider to be most important. Place an "X" before the three you believe to be least important.

1–2–3–X

_____ 1. _____ of the delegates to the Constitutional Convention had attended the Continental Congress

_____ 2. The Founding Fathers averaged just over _____ years of age.

_____ 3. Benjamin Franklin was _____ years old in 1878.

_____ 4. According to the Constitution, _____ slaves were considered the equivalent of three citizens, each slave was defined as _____ of a person.

_____ 5. The survey of western land created townships _____ miles square divided into 36 sections of _____ acres each.

_____ 6. By 1781 it took almost $ _____ paper dollars to purchase what one dollar in gold would bring.

For those three which you have chosen as most important, give reasons and evidence to support your choices.

a. _____

_____

_____

b. _____

_____

_____

c. _____

_____

_____

IV. Concepts–Ideas

Identify each of the following key words briefly and explain the relationship between them and the words that follow in parentheses.

1. convention (secret — revolutionary — methodical — one faction)

_____

_____

2. delegates (economic class — experience — students — young children of the Revolution — national)

_____

_____

3. state taxes (farmers — mortgages — harassment — Shays — "tree of liberty" — order and stability)

_____

_____

4. conservatism (great beast — tradition — institutions — check democracy)

_____

_____

5. mixed government (Adams — Massachusetts — three principles — checks and balances)

_____

_____

6. federal (central government — state governments — accommodation — Great Compromise — local interests)

_____

_____

7. Anti-Federalists (majority — tyranny — small countries — *The Federalist Papers*)

_____

_____

8. sovereignty of the people (written constitutions — popular ratification — annual elections — weak governors)

_____

_____

9. right to vote (few excluded — Christian — males — property qualifications — residency)

_____

_____

10. confederation (alliance of states — no executive — not regulate trade — built-in weaknesses)

_____

_____

Which two concepts are most controversial in the contemporary world? Explain why.

a. _____

_____

_____

b. _____

_____

_____

V. Essay Questions

Write notes under each of the following questions that would help you answer similar essay questions on an exam.

1. Explain the arguments against the Constitution by the anti-Federalists.

   _____

   _____

   _____

2. Rank the first ten amendments to the Constitution in order of their importance. Explain your ranking.

   _____

   _____

   _____

3. Are the checks, limits, and balances at the heart of the constitution a hindrance to efficiency and to passing the best laws? Why or why not?

   _____

   _____

   _____

4. Should the Supreme Court have been allowed to develop its power of "judicial review" since it was not written into the Constitution? Explain.

   _____

   _____

   _____

5. What important decisions were made in the formation of state constitutions, 1776–78? Were these actions just as important as writing a national constitution? Why or why not?

   _____

   _____

   _____

6. Describe the political and economic problems in the United States in the 1780s. Were these so serious that only a new constitution could overcome them? Explain.

   _____

   _____

   _____

7. Which of the two men do you consider to be the most important in establishing a strong United States—George Washington or Alexander Hamilton? Explain your choice.

   _____

   _____

   _____

8. Describe the characteristics of the Founding Fathers. Which single characteristic stands out as most important? Explain.

_____

_____

9. Consider the whole process of constitution-making from calling the convention to the completion of ratification. What pitfalls or obstructions might have kept it from being so successful? Be specific, but use your imagination.

_____

_____

10. What was undemocratic—revealed a fear of democracy—in the process of establishing a constitution and in the document itelf? Be specific.

_____

_____

11. React to the statement that "property alone gave a person a stake in society and therefore qualified him to govern it." Do you agree or disagree? Why?

_____

_____

_____

VI. Determining Relevance of Data

Examine each of the following statements about the process of forming the Constitution, and in the blank before each statement, write a "VR" if the statement is *very relevant* to our understanding of its formation and an "LR" if the item is *less relevant*.

VR–LR

_____ 1. Hamilton was an unabashed admirer of English culture and government.

_____ 2. John Adams was ambassador to Great Britain and did not attend the constitutional Convention.

_____ 3. The word "slave" does not appear in the Constitution.

_____ 4. *Technically*, New York's vote on ratification of the Constitution was "no."

_____ 5. The delegates met in Philadelphia on hot, humid summer days.

_____ 6. Jefferson did not attend the Constitutional Convention and commented on Shays' Rebellion by saying, "A little rebellion now and then is a good thing."

_____ 7. The basic principle of the American Constitution is a complex arrangement of checks and balances.

_____ 8. The series of meetings that eventually led to the Convention began because of a squabble over oysters, crabs, and flounder.

_____ 9. Benjamin Franklin, a delegate, was 81 years old in 1787.

_____ 10. The delegates celebrated in a tavern after their work was finished in September 1787.

_____ 11. Madison believed that the key to preserving liberties was a balanced government, and he had his way.

_____ 12. Washington and Hamilton, as conservatives of the time, were suspicious of human nature and therefore supported a strong, active, central government.

VII. Fact–Judgment

Determine whether you consider each of the following statements to be a fact (F) or a judgment (J). A judgment may be true and you may agree with it, but it remains a judgment because it is _derived from_ fact and not a fact itself. It could be either a reasoned judgment or a professional interpretation. Write your choice in the blank to the left of the statement.

F–J

_____ 1. The Founding Fathers suspected the human race and feared its darker side.

_____ 2. The Constitution has been a remarkably successful basic law, and the generation of political leaders who wrote and debated it were rich in talent and wisdom.

_____ 3. The Constitutional Convention met in secret from first to last.

_____ 4. Never had a nation been founded so methodically.

_____ 5. Europe's refusal to recognize the United States as a nation was a major reason for the Founding Fathers' decision to redesign their government.

_____ 6. Under the Articles of Confederation some of the thirteen states adopted tariffs that discriminated against the goods produced by other states.

_____ 7. Uncontrolled democracy leads to despotism.

_____ 8. In the American Revolution, Americans had defended tradition against a reckless, radical Parliament that had run roughshod over it.

_____ 9. In Pennsylvania, the Federalists managed ratification only by physically forcing two anti-Federalist members to remain in their seats.

_____ 10. The anti-Federalists (those opposed to the Constitution) may have represented the views of the majority of Americans.

_____ 11. The Founding Fathers assumed that the civil liberties of citizens were accounted for in the lists of rights most states included in their basic laws.

_____ 12. The supreme court of Massachusetts ruled that slavery was unconstitutional there because their constitution stated that "all men are born free and equal."

_____ 13. The economy of the 1780s suffered from the termination of privileges that Americans had enjoyed as British subjects.

_____ 14. The Northwest Ordinance defined the status of territories as self-governing states in the making.

_____ 15. In the Act of 1787, slavery was forbidden in the territories north of the Ohio River.

ANSWERS

I. True–False	II. Multiple Choice	III. Quantification	VI. Determining Relevance of Data		VII. Fact–Judgment
1. True	1. c	1. 39	1.	VR	1. F
2. False	2. b	2. 40	2.	LR	2. J
3. False	3. d	3. 81; 40	3.	LR	3. F
4. False	4. c	4. 5; three-fifths	4.	LR	4. J
5. False	5. b	5. 6; 640	5.	LR	5. J
6. True	6. a	6. 150	6.	VR	6. F
7. False	7. d		7.	VR	7. J
8. True			8.	LR	8. J
9. True			9.	LR	9. F
10. True			10.	LR	10. J
			11.	VR	11. F
			12.	VR	12. F
					13. J
					14. F
					15. F

⊨11⊨

We the People

Putting the Constitution to Work
1789–1800

*"A jug sat on every shop counter; every general
store doubled as a saloon."*

"History is a pageant, not a philosophy."

Augustine Burell

I. **True–False**
If the statement is false, change any words necessary to make it true.

_____ 1. Only two candidates ran against George Washington in 1792.

_____ 2. Hamilton and Washington changed their view of the French Revolution when Lafayette sent Washington the key to the Bastille.

_____ 3. Washington was so enraged by the activities of Citizen Genêt that he ordered him to return to France.

_____ 4. In New England wealthy people were generally pro-French and anti-British because of trade competition with the British.

_____ 5. John Jay had to resign his seat on the Supreme Court because of his unpopular treaty.

_____ 6. There were many religious crusades against whiskey on the frontier in the 1790s.

_____ 7. Wealthy people were inclined to be Federalists, especially the urban wealthy.

_____ 8. Abigail Adams was a principal advisor of her husband John Adams when he was president.

_____ 9. Although the Sedition Act was dangerous to the Bill of Rights, it was never really enforced.

II. Multiple Choice

_____ 1. In his farewell address Washington focused on

    a. signing helpful alliances with foreign nations

    b. forming only two political parties

    c. being proud of the section in which you live

    d. voicing opposition through peaceful and legal channels

_____ 2. The cabinet member who supported the French Revolution most was

    a. Jefferson

    b. Hamilton

    c. Washington

    d. Jay

_____ 3. Jay's Treaty of 1794 with England called for all but which of the following:

    a. evacuation of the western forts

    b. compensation of American shipowners for losses in the West Indies

    c. Americans pledged not to discriminate against British shipping

    d. the British would stop the imprisonment of American seamen

_____ 4. The westerners used corn whiskey for all but which of the following reasons?

    a. money

    b. for fattening cattle

    c. with their meals

    d. medicine for malaria

_____ 5. Pinckney's Treaty was important to westerners because

    a. it opened the Mississippi to American navigation

    b. it assured the statehood of Kentucky

    c. it forbade storage of goods at New Orleans

    d. it contained claims regarding Indian lands

_____ 6. John Adams displayed all but which of the following characteristics:

    a. furious temper

    b. dishonesty

    c. intolerance

    d. pomposity

_____ 7. Both Jefferson and Madison wrote resolutions against

    a. the French seizure of American ships

    b. the Alien and Sedition Acts

    c. the XYZ Affair

    d. the Irish rebels in America

III. Quantification

Fill in each blank in the following statements with the correct number or numbers. In the blank at the left check the _five_ statements that you consider to be the most significant in understanding the topics in the chapter.

_____ 1. Citizen Genêt's American privateers seized _____ British merchantmen and awarded them as prizes to the captors.

_____ 2. During 1793 and 1794 British warships seized _____ American vessels, many in sight of American beaches.

_____ 3. William Henry Harrison said that he "saw more drunk men in _____ hours ... in Cincinnati than I had in my previous life."

_____ 4. A horse that could carry only four bushels of grain could carry the equivalent of _____ bushels if it had been transformed into liquor.

_____ 5. By the time Adams took the oath of office, the French had seized _____ American vessels.

_____ 6. Under the Sedition Act, Federalists indicted and convicted _____ important Republican newspaper editors for seditious words.

_____ 7. Only _____ states elected presidential electors by popular vote in 1796.

IV. Concepts–Ideas

Identify each of the following key words briefly and explain the relationship between them and the words that follow in parentheses.

1. equality and fraternity (French Revolution — end social distinctions — too fast — liberty)

_____

_____

2. alliance (technical obligations — invalid — French monarchy — England aggressor)

_____

_____

3. Rule of 1756 (neutral trade — French West Indies — invited — footstuffs)

_____

_____

4. privateers (private vessels — wage war — pirates — navy)

_____

_____

5. drinkers (malaria — medicine — isolation — jug — percolating still)

_____

_____

6. parties (Republican — Federalist — urban rich — coastal areas — farmers — foreign policy)

_____

_____

7. electors (independent — popular vote — legislature — vote for two — manipulation)

_____

_____

8. invective (Bache — debauched — legalize corruption — usurper — political iniquity)

_____

_____

9. bribery (tribute — diplomacy — insult — humiliation — undeclared war)

_____

_____

10. sedition (fines and prison — "contempt or disrepute" — convictions — resolutions)

_____

_____

11. childbirth (mid-wife — seven times — communal — practical — feminine — Eve — jokes — fever — touch)

_____

_____

12. office of the president (dignified — best and brightest — a crown — regal carriage — precedents)

_____

_____

13. funding debt (face value — speculator — enrich capitalists — future lenders)

_____

_____

14. national bank (private enterprise — government finances — fees and interest — unconstitutional)

_____

_____

V. Essay Questions

Write notes under each of the following questions that would help you answer similar essay questions on an exam.

1. Describe life on the log cabin frontier.

_____

_____

_____

2. Do you agree or disagree with the Virginia and Kentucky Resolutions? Why?

_____

_____

_____

3. Which was more of a threat to the American political system—the Whiskey Rebellion or the Sedition Act? Explain your choice.

_____

_____

_____

4. Compare and contrast the election of 1796 to the election of 1800. Point out similarities and differences.

_____

_____

_____

5. What were the important differences in the Republican and the Federalist parties?

_____

_____

_____

6. List the provisions of Jay's Treaty and Pinckney's Treaty. Which was the most successful? Explain why.

_____

_____

_____

7. Describe the problems involved in American reaction to the French Revolution. Be thorough and specific.

_____

_____

_____

8. Because of the Treaty of 1778, the French aid in our revolution, and the similarity of our styles of government, should the United States have supported France in her European wars in the 1790s? Why or why not?

_____

_____

_____

9. Describe the policies of Secretary of the Treasury Alexander Hamilton and explain the reasons for his proposals. Do you agree or disagree with Hamilton's ideas? Why?

_____

_____

_____

10. What were the major objections to Hamilton's programs? Were these, in your opinion, valid objections? Explain.

_____

_____

_____

VI. Ranking

Rank the following events, developments, and decisions from 1 to 10 according to your assessment of their importance in the 1790s. Consider their consequences, their precedents, their implications at the time and in the long run. The most important would be 1, and least important would be 10.

1–10

_____ a. Washington's decision to support the unpopular Jay's Treaty and keep the United States out of a war with Britain.

_____ b. The effort by the French to obtain a bribe before negotiating with American diplomats.

_____ c. Washington's vigorous suppression of the Whiskey Rebellion.

_____ d. The vote in the 1800 election by the House of Representatives in favor of Jefferson as president.

_____ e. Adams' refusal, despite the pressure of his party, to go to war with France despite the French seizure of American ships and efforts to obtain bribes.

_____ f. The death of George Washington in 1799, which brought all political factions together in mourning at the height of the Sedition Act controversy.

_____ g. General Anthony Wayne's victory over the Miamis and Shawnees at the Battle of Fallen Timbers in 1794.

_____ h. Pinckney's Treaty opening the Mississippi River to American navigation and granting the "right of deposit" in New Orleans.

_____ i. The activities of Citizen Genêt in outfitting American privateers to prey upon British shipping.

_____ j. Marquis de Lafayette's gift of the key from the Bastille to George Washington.

1. For the two choices that you gave the highest rank, explain why you consider them the most important.

a. . _____

_____

_____

b. _____

_____

_____

2. For the choice you gave the lowest rank, explain why you consider it the least important.

_____

_____

_____

VII. Fact–Judgment

Determine whether you consider each of the following statements to be a fact (F) or a judgment (J). A judgment may be true and you may agree with it, but it remains a judgment because it is *derived from* a fact and not a fact itself. It could be either a reasoned judgment or a professional interpretation. Write your choice in the blank to the left of the statement.

F–J

_____ 1. Washington regarded political parties as unions of selfish people with narrow interests.

_____ 2. American clergymen realized that the French revolutionary, Robespierre, was attacking not just the Catholic Church but all religion.

_____ 3. Regarding the war in Europe, Washington announced that the United States would be neutral, "impartial toward the belligerent powers."

_____ 4. The British proclaimed that neutral nations could not trade in enemy ports from which they had been excluded before the war.

_____ 5. American merchants grew rich on the French trade and built elegant town houses whose architectural style has come to be known as Federal.

_____ 6. In Jay's Treaty, Americans pledged not to discriminate against British shipping and to pay debts owed to British subjects incurred before the Revolution.

_____ 7. Washington, along with wealthy planters and merchants, were deeply involved in land speculation in the Northwest Territory.

_____ 8. In the 1790s the local preacher was likely to match his congregation in drinking whiskey.

_____ 9. Washington called the leaders of the Whiskey Rebellion "mental defectives," his way of showing his contempt for rebels of every kind.

_____ 10. Thomas Jefferson was unmistakably the Republican leader, although James Madison's energy and wise counsel was indispensable to their cause.

_____ 11. John Adams was extremely unpleasant to know and to work with.

_____ 12. Washington's agreement to command an army against France humiliated Adams and caused him to worry about a military coup.

_____ 13. The Third Alien Act allowed the president to deport any foreigner whom he deemed "dangerous to the peace and safety of the United States."

_____ 14. No other state legislatures adopted the Kentucky and Virginia Resolutions.

_____ 15. The 1800 election crisis between Jefferson and Burr proved that parties were a fact in American life.

_____ 16. Citizen Genêt was young, bombastic, and devoid of a sense of diplomacy.

_____ 17. The Fifth Amendment is the basis of the citizen's right to refuse to testify in a trial in which he or she is a defendant.

_____ 18. Hamilton soon emerged as the most powerful figure in the cabinet.

_____ 19. Several dozen congressmen who stood to profit directly from Hamilton's funding bill voted for it and helped get it passed.

_____ 20. In raising its armies, the Revolution wrenched thousands of young men from their homes and accustomed ways of life at a critical time in their lives.

VIII. Chronology

Number the following events in their correct chronological order from 1 to 10.

1–10

_____ a. Battle of Fallen Timbers

_____ b. Jay's Treaty with England

_____ c. XYZ Affair

_____ d. Sedition Act

_____ e. Washington's announcement of American neutrality

_____ f. Virginia and Kentucky Resolutions

_____ g. Whiskey Rebellion

_____ h. Jefferson elected President

_____ i. Citizen Genêt commissioned American "privateers"

_____ j. election of John Adams as president

IX. Choosing What Is Important

Determine whether you consider each of the following statements to be very important (VI) or less important (LI). Write your choice in the blank to the left of each statement.

VI–LI

_____ 1. Washington and Hamilton were not happy with the movement of the French Revolution from liberty to the principles of equality and fraternity.

_____ 2. Hamilton argued that the treaty of 1778 with France was invalid because it had been made with the French monarchy that no longer existed.

_____ 3. During the early stages of the French Revolution, it was declared that everyone was to be addressed as "Citizen" and "Citizeness."

_____ 4. With British seizure of American ships, shipowners lost only property; sailors sacrificed their freedom and sometimes their lives.

_____ 5. John Jay hobnobbed happily in English high society and even kissed the hand of King George's queen.

VI–LI

_____ 6. The treaty of John Jay marked the beginning of the first American party system—Federalists versus Jefferson Republicans.

_____ 7. The death rate on the frontier was high due to the killing labor, infectious disease, malnutrition, and Indian battles.

_____ 8. In the west a jug of whiskey sat on every shop's counter; every general store doubled as a saloon.

_____ 9. Hamilton led perhaps half the Federalists in Congress, and he neither liked nor much respected Adams.

_____ 10. None of the three Alien Acts were enforced, although many foreigners fled the United States for fear that they would be.

_____ 11. In a series of resolutions, Madison and Jefferson declared that the states possessed the power to overrule the unconstitutional actions of Congress.

_____ 12. Hamilton, the Federalist, pressured a few Federalist congressmen to abstain, thus giving the 1800 election to Jefferson.

ANSWERS

I. True–False	II. Multiple Choice	III. Quantification		VII. Fact–Judgment	VIII. Chronology	
1. False	1. d	1.	80	1. F	a.	5
2. False	2. a	2.	600	2. J	b.	4
3. True	3. d	3.	48	3. F	c.	7
4. False	4. b	4.	24	4. F	d.	8
5. True	5. a	5.	300	5. F	e.	2
6. False	6. b	6.	4	6. F	f.	9
7. True	7. b	7.	6	7. F	g.	1
8. True				8. J	h.	10
9. False				9. J	i.	3
10. True				10. J	j.	6
				11. J		
				12. J		

IX. Choosing What is Important

1.	LI	
2.	VI	13. F
3.	LI	14. F
4.	VI	15. J
5.	LI	16. J
6.	VI	17. F
7.	LI	18. J
8.	LI	19. F
9.	VI	20. J
10.	LI	
11.	VI	
12.	VI	

The Age of Thomas Jefferson

Expansion at Home, Frustration Abroad, 1800–1815

"Every difference of opinion is not a difference in principle.... We have called by different names brethren of the same principle."

Thomas Jefferson

"I hold it a noble task to rescue from oblivion those who deserve to be eternally remembered."

Pliny the Younger

I. True–False
If the statement is false, change any words necessary to make it true.

_____ 1. Thomas Jefferson's Republicans were the ancestors of the present-day Republican party.

_____ 2. Alexander Hamilton considered Jefferson soft-headed and frivolous.

_____ 3. Jefferson believed that the majority of the people would do the correct thing; if they did not, their will should be followed nevertheless.

_____ 4. Supreme Court Justice Samuel Chase became the first judge to be found guilty by the Senate in an impeachment trial.

_____ 5. Jefferson wrote privately about the Louisiana Purchase that what was practicable must control, oftentimes, what is pure theory.

_____ 6. Alexander Hamilton killed Aaron Burr, then vice-president, in a duel over Burr's integrity and Hamilton's adultery.

_____ 7. As justification for impressment of seamen, the British argued that British birth made a person a lifelong British subject.

_____ 8. The War Hawks were children of the nation rather than its founders, and thus were intensely nationalistic.

_____ 9. In August 1814, the British burned the Capitol and the White House.

_____ 10. The Treaty of Ghent (ending the war with Great Britain) was signed before the Battle of New Orleans was fought.

II. Multiple Choice

_____ 1. Thomas Jefferson did all but which of the following:

   a. spoke several foreign languages
   b. invented bifocals
   c. invented the swivel chair
   d. smuggled a variety of rice out of Italy.

_____ 2. The National Republicans were

   a. a new name for the Federalist party
   b. soon to become Jackson's party
   c. the party of John Quincy Adams
   d. later to be the party of liberals

_____ 3. Jefferson did only one of the following:

   a. followed normal rules of protocol
   b. served meals himself at small parties
   c. dabbled in everything *except* science
   d. founded William and Mary College

_____ 4. Lewis and Clark traveled along all the following rivers except the

   a. Platte River
   b. Missouri River
   c. Salmon River
   d. Columbia River

_____ 5. Macon's Bill No. 2 stipulated that the United States would

   a. trade with England and France but cut off trade with the nation that did not agree to American terms
   b. not receive a French or British ambassador
   c. not trade with nations that traded with the British
   d. declare war unless trade continued

_____ 6. Sections favoring the War of 1812 against the British were the

   a. Northeast
   b. states of New York and Florida
   c. South, West, and Pennsylvania
   d. South only

_____ 7. The Embargo Act of 1807 harmed the interests of all but which of the following:

   a. American shipping interests
   b. Federalist party
   c. farmers
   d. New England merchants

III. Quantification

Fill in each blank in the following statements with the correct number of numbers. Then determine whether you consider the statement to be very important (VI) or less important (LI). Write your choice in the blank to the left of each statement.

VI–LI

_____ 1. On the day before he left office, the Federalist John Adams appointed _____ Federalists to the federal judiciary.

_____ 2. By 1800, almost _____ Americans lived in the western states and each year they shipped _____ tons of produce down the Mississippi.

_____ 3. Through the 1790s, the price of sailing in Barbary waters cost the American Treasury about $ _____ million.

_____ 4. In 1807, at the height of the commerce raiding, Massachusetts merchants earned $ _____ million in freight charges alone.

_____ 5. In one year the British seized _____ Americans ships and the French seized about _____ .

_____ 6. The pay to sailors on American merchant ships was as much as _____ that on British ships, thus British seamen made up about _____ the total crew on American ships.

_____ 7. About _____ native-born Americans were forced into the Royal Navy during the Napoleonic Wars.

_____ 8. Federalist and mercantile states voted _____ to _____ against the War of 1812 while the South, West, and Pennsylvania voted _____ to _____ in favor.

_____ 9. At the Battle of New Orleans _____ Britons fell dead while Jackson lost _____ men.

Which two statistics do you consider most significant? Explain.

a. _____
_____
_____

b. _____
_____
_____

IV. Concepts–Ideas

Identify each of the following key words briefly and explain the relationship between them and the words that follow in parentheses.

1. embargo (ballast — no purchases — farmers — New England — costs)

_____

_____

2. impressment ("press gangs" — draft merchantmen — triple pay — citizenship — naturalization)

_____

_____

3. cold war (crippled economy — neutral trade — "license" — French seizure — profits)

_____

_____

4. conspiracy (secession — treason — Burr — unknown plans — acquittal)

_____

_____

5. "protection money" (Tripoli — buy passage — indignant — gifts of friendship — payments)

_____

_____

6. exploration (overland trade route — Indian tribes — Pacific — plant and animal life — no battles)

_____

_____

7. territorial purchase (constitutional — citizenship — hypocrite — right of deposit — _L'Ouverture_)

_____

_____

8. unconstitutional (writ of mandamus — powers of Congress — judge the law — impeachment)

_____

_____

9. simplicity (no pomp — ignore protocol — small parties — slippers — rooming house)

_____

_____

10. old traditions (Tecumseh — Prophet — warrior — grafted Christianity — books — sell land)

_____

_____

V. Essay Questions

Write notes under each of the following questions that would help you answer similar essay questions on an exam.

1. Describe in some detail the background and activity of Tecumseh and the Prophet. What aspects of their lives and beliefs are symbolic of the problems of relations between Indians and whites in America? Explain.

_____

_____

_____

2. In what ways could the War of 1812 be called a useless, unnecessary, futile war? Explain your answer.

_____

_____

_____

3. Explain both the British and the American viewpoints on the issue of impressment of seamen.

_____

_____

_____

4. Describe the attempts of Jefferson and Madison to deal with the British and French policy and action regarding neutral trade in the Atlantic. In your opinion what policy should have been followed? Explain.

_____

_____

_____

5. Why was the career of Aaron Burr "tragic and comic?" In what ways might the man be called dangerous? Explain.

_____

_____

_____

6. List and explain the findings and results of the Lewis and Clark expedition of 1804–1806. Which result was the most important? Why?

_____

_____

_____

7. Was Jefferson correct in his choice to forget his principles and agree to the purchase of the Louisiana Territory? Or should he have, as a man of integrity, remained attached to his principles regardless of the circumstances or opportunity? Should practical considerations modify and alter political principles? Explain.

_____

_____

_____

8. Describe Jefferson's style of life as president. Was this a style more fitting a democracy than Washington's style? Why or why not?

_____

_____

_____

9. Would you consider Thomas Jefferson a great president? Why or why not? Give specific evidence for your answer. How would you rank him with Washington, Adams, and Madison? Explain the reasons for your ranking.

_____

_____

_____

10. Without looking at your textbook, draw a map of North America as it looked in 1803. Include the states, territories, rivers, and non-United States possessions. (Check your drawing with the map in the text.)

11. What was "giving birth" like in the Federalist and Jeffersonian eras? How do ideas about childbirth differ in the contemporary world?

_____

_____

_____

VI. Ranking

Rank the following events and decisions from 1 to 10 according to your assessment of their importance. The most important would be 1, and the least important would be 10.

1–10

_____ a. Lewis and Clark expedition

_____ b. Purchase of Louisiana Territory

_____ c. Marbury vs. Madison court decision

_____ d. Harrison's victory at Tippecanoe

_____ e. Jackson's victory at the Battle of New Orleans

_____ f. British burn the Capitol and the White House

1–10

_____ g. Jefferson's Embargo Act

_____ h. Burr's conspiracy to lead a secession of the western states and territory

_____ i. Jefferson's decision to give in and pay the Barbary pirates

_____ j. Madison's decision to ask Congress for a declaration of war against the British

For the two choices you gave the highest rank, explain why you consider them the most important.

a. _____

_____

_____

b. _____

_____

_____

VII. Fact–Judgment–Importance

Determine whether you consider each of the following statements to be a fact (F) or a judgment (J). A judgment may be true and you may agree with it, but it remains a judgment because it is *derived from* fact and not a fact itself. It could be either a reasoned judgment or a professional interpretation. For those statements you consider to be very important, label (VI) or less important (LI). Write your choices in the blanks to the left of the statement.

F–J   VI–LI

_____ _____ 1. Jefferson wrote better English than any president except Abraham Lincoln.

_____ _____ 2. Jefferson believed that all men had the same rights but not all possessed equal abilities.

_____ _____ 3. As president, Jefferson proved even more willing to stretch his powers beyond the letter of the law.

_____ _____ 4. Jefferson pardoned the people who were still imprisoned under the Sedition Act, reduced the residency requirements for citizenship, and slashed government expenditures.

_____ _____ 5. When in 1803, Napoleon realized that his dream of a great American Empire was lost for good after his defeat at Santo Domingo, he said "Damn sugar" and "Damn colonies."

_____ _____ 6. Regarding constitutional questions, Jefferson instructed his supporters in Congress that "the less we say about constitutional difficulties respecting Louisiana the better."

_____ _____ 7. Lewis and Clark found that one of the favorite expressions of the Indians of the Northwest coast was "son of a beech."

_____ _____ 8. Ohio became the seventeenth state in 1803 and, voting Republican like Kentucky and Tennessee, enabled Jefferson to win reelection easily in 1804.

_____ _____ 9. In 1804 Burr, possessed of manic energy and keen imagination, turned his gaze toward Louisiana.

F–J   VI–LI

_____ _____ 10. England paid "protection money" to Barbary pirates, considering it cheaper to buy free passage than to make war.

_____ _____ 11. Under Napoleon's Continental System, neutral ships that observed the British trade stipulations would be seized by the French.

_____ _____ 12. The Embargo was a logical action for Jefferson, who in his revolutionary youth had seen nonimportation bring Parliament around.

_____ _____ 13. More important to the War Hawks than British depredations on American shipping was their outrage at "the injuries and indignities" heaped on the United States by British arrogance.

_____ _____ 14. One American general in the invasion of Canada was so fat he could not ride a horse but had to be hauled around in a special cart.

_____ _____ 15. President Madison barely escaped capture when, at a battle he went to view, the American army fled without fighting.

_____ _____ 16. After the Battle of New Orleans, Jackson hanged as many American soldiers for desertion as were killed during the battle.

_____ _____ 17. Most singers have said that Francis Scott Key did the nation no favor by choosing as the music for his lyrics a popular English drinking song.

_____ _____ 18. After Jackson's victory, the defeat of the Creek Indians in the Southeast, and Decatur's victory in Algiers, Americans could feel that they had taken their rightful place in the world.

ANSWERS

I. True–False	**II. Multiple Choice**	**III. Quantification**			**VIII. Fact–Judgment–Importance**		
1. False	1. b	LI	1.	42	1.	J	LI
2. True	2. c	VI	2.	400,000; 20,000	2.	F	VI
3. True	3. b	LI	3.	2	3.	F	VI
4. False	4. a	LI	4.	15	4.	F	VI
5. True	5. a	VI	5.	1,000; 500	5.	F	LI
6. False	6. c	VI	6.	triple; half	6.	F	VI
7. True	7. b	VI	7.	10,000	7.	F	LI
8. True		VI	8.	34; 14; 65; 15	8.	J	VI
9. True		LI	9.	2,000; 7	9.	J	LI
10. True					10.	F	LI
					11.	F	VI
					12.	J	LI
					13.	J	VI
					14.	F	LI
					15.	F	LI
					16.	F	LI
					17.	J	LI
					18	J	VI

⇌13⇌

Beyond the Appalachian Ridge

The West in the Early Nineteenth Century

"In the United States, a man builds a house in which to spend his old age, and he sells it before the roof is on."

Alexis de Tocqueville

"The aim of the historian, like that of the artist, is to enlarge our picture of the world, to give us a new way of looking at things."

James Joll

I. **True–False**
If the statement is false, change any words necessary to make it true.

_____ 1. Americans seemed to be a people who could put down roots on a good farm and hold it for generations.

_____ 2. By 1820 the United States had some roads that were surfaced with crushed rock or macadam.

_____ 3. Henry Clay not only promoted the War of 1812 but later went to Ghent, Belgium, to help draw up a peace treaty to end it.

_____ 4. Improvements in transportation under the American system were to be paid for by excise taxes and cotton sales.

_____ 5. The Mainline Canal in Pennsylvania was even more successful than the Erie Canal because of its shorter route.

_____ 6. The Baltimore and Ohio Railroad was started in 1828 and completed in five years.

_____ 7. A steamship had to carry its own fuel and was looked upon as inferior to a sailing ship that could be loaded entirely with saleable merchandise.

_____ 8. In the Kentucky long rifle the ball had to be wrapped in greased linen or a leather patch so that compression was established and the bullet took the rifling.

_____ 9. Nearly everyone who had money to spare in the West was attracted to land speculation and the inevitability of rising value.

_____ 10. A squatter was a westerner who drove legitimate settlers off their land and then sold it illegally.

II. Multiple Choice

_____ 1. The man who spoke for the small farmer in the West (and who once shot Andrew Jackson in a duel) was:

a. Thomas Hart Benton
b. Henry Clay
c. James Fitch
d. Eli Whitney

_____ 2. In 1824 when Jackson ran for president, how many of the 24 states were in the West?

a. 3
b. 5
c. 2
d. 9

_____ 3. In the 1804 Jefferson land sale plan, a farmer could buy 160 acres with a minimum down payment of

a. $240
b. $80
c. $4
d. $160

_____ 4. Most speculators went West with a little money and the intent to

a. buy a farm and settle down
b. set up shop in a small town
c. buy land cheap and sell it dear
d. sell supplies at a high price to other settlers

_____ 5. The greatest danger in riding steamboats on the Mississippi was

a. sand bars
b. sly gamblers
c. boiler explosions
d. bandits on rafts

_____ 6. A technique used by railway entrepreneurs to avoid use by other companies was to

a. build different gauges of track
b. guard both ends of the line
c. set traps on curves for rival trains
d. all of the above

_____ 7. The oddity about Henry Clay's willingness to take part in duels was that

a. he hated the sight of blood
b. his arthritis prevented him from pulling a trigger
c. he was a poor shot
d. he never actually fired at his opponent

III. Quantification

Fill in each blank in the following statements with the correct number or numbers. Then determine whether you consider the statement to be very important (VI) or less important (LI). Write your choice in the blank to the left of each statement.

VI–LI

_____ 1. By 1830, fully _____ percent of the American people lived west of the Appalachians.

_____ 2. By 1820, there were _____ miles of toll roads (turnpikes) in the United States.

_____ 3. The cost of shipping goods along the Erie Canal was _____ percent cheaper than the overland route.

_____ 4. By 1848 there were more than _____ miles of railroad in the United States, more than _____ the total track in all other countries combined.

_____ 5. In 1812 it took _____ weeks to float a cargo from Cincinnati to New York, but by 1852, by rail, it took no more than _____ days.

_____ 6. Before the steamboat it took _____ weeks to float a cargo from Pittsburgh to New Orleans but _____ months to bring a smaller tonnage back.

_____ 7. Robert Fulton's steamboat had a great advantage over sailing ships in that it drew only _____ feet of water.

_____ 8. Even in the most practiced hands, the long rifle fired only about _____ times out of _____ .

_____ 9. Stunned by the Panic of 1819, Congress abolished credit purchases of land in 1820 and reduced the minimum tract to _____ acres and the minimum price per acre to $ _____ .

IV. Concepts –Ideas

Identify each of the following key words briefly and explain the relationship between them and the words that follow in parentheses.

1. moving (no roots — inns and stables — dizzying sell and go — antisocial — boosters)

_____

_____

2. isolation (markets — manufactures — walk — animal trails — cost — tax)

_____

_____

3. internal improvements (federal construction — promotion — Clay — National Road — taxation — unconstitutional — manipulators — emigration)

_____

_____

4. continentalism (turn inward — market in West — financing — tariff — food products — cotton)

_____

_____

5. canal craze (expensive — bottlenecks — slow — ill-advised — bankruptcy — no internal improvements)

_____

_____

6. railroads (any weather — up mountains — fast — reliable — safe — versatile — unromantic)

_____

_____

7. river transport (steamboats — explode — shallow water — race — cordwood — upstream)

_____

_____

8. speculation (risks — "sharpers" — "inevitability" — "cultivators" — down payment — "wildcat banks" — paper money)

_____

_____

9. panic (gullibility — "greater fool" — loans due — sell out — banks close — revert to government)

_____

_____

10. preemption (squatter — minimum price — graduation — development — tax rolls — magnetic attraction)

_____

_____

V. Essay Questions

Write notes under each of the following questions that would help you answer similar essay questions on an exam.

1. Describe a characteristic of the American people facing the open West. Is this a desirable trait? To what extent is it still with us?

_____

_____

_____

2. Was Henry Clay a man of vision in his conception of the American System or was he unfair to the South? Explain.

_____

_____

_____

3. Explain how the American System was supposed to help each section of the nation. Are delicate economic programs such as Clay's unrealistic?

_____

_____

_____

4. Why was the Erie Canal so successful and other canals failures?

_____

_____

_____

5. What were the successes and problems of early railroads from 1828 to 1860?

_____

_____

_____

6. Describe the development of the steamboat from 1787 to 1841. What were the most difficult problems to overcome?

_____

_____

_____

7. Explain the activities of land speculators. Should they be considered harmful characters seeking a profit at any cost or catalysts and enablers for the rapid settlement of the West?

_____

_____

_____

8. What were the causes of the Panic of 1819? Should the government have anticipated it and altered its policies? Why or why not?

_____

_____

_____

9. Jefferson helped bring about the Panic of 1819 by his shortsighted land policy. Is this statement accurate or a wide exaggeration? Explain.

_____

_____

10. What were the similarities and differences of Thomas Hart Benton and Henry Clay? Which of the two men do you most admire?

_____

_____

11. What was "life on the frontier" like in the early nineteenth century? What features of this life continue today in our imagery of the West, the frontier, and rural communities?

_____

_____

_____

VI. Fact–Judgment–Importance

Determine whether you consider each of the following statements to be a fact (F) or a judgment (J). A judgment may be true and you may agree with it, but it remains a judgment because it is *derived from* fact and not a fact itself. It could be either a reasoned judgment or a professional interpretation. Then decide whether each statement is very important (VI) or less important (LI). Write your choice in the blank to the left of the statement.

F–J   VI–LI

_____ _____ 1. In as much as opportunity was synonymous with America, the West became the symbol of the United States.

_____ _____ 2. Town boosters laid out marketing centers complete with street names before a single tree had been felled.

_____ _____ 3. Only the federal government could afford to spend money to build roads without the prospect of immediate returns.

_____ _____ 4. Henry Clay charmed women with his good looks and wit, and appealed to men with his card playing and dueling pistol.

_____ _____ 5. New Englanders tended to look abroad rather than to the far-off West for their economic life.

_____ _____ 6. Southerners needed no help in finding markets for their cotton in Manchester and Leeds, England.

_____ _____ 7. As a result of the Erie Canal, New York City outstripped Philadelphia to become the country's largest city.

F–J   VI–LI

_____ _____ 8. Most of the 4,000 miles of canals that were dug in imitation of the Erie Canal were ill-advised.

_____ _____ 9. Competitive jealousies among railroad companies worked against the realization of an efficient network that would connect distant points.

_____ _____ 10. Both canals and railroads tended to link the West with the Northeast.

_____ _____ 11. For more than a century after the perfection of the steamship, clipper ships and the steel-hulled windjammers dominated many world trade routes.

_____ _____ 12. The military and militarty posts stimulated settlement on some frontiers.

_____ _____ 13. Federalist land policy favored speculators, but the Jeffersonian policy was designed to help the cultivators.

_____ _____ 14. Settlers often found themselves priced out of the market by speculators who would pay high prices with paper money hoping to resell at still higher prices.

_____ _____ 15. In some areas squatters combated speculators with vigilante actions.

_____ _____ 16. Benton became the West's leading voice for hard money over paper money.

_____ _____ 17. Benton's easy policy with land sales would promote the development of the West and get more land on tax rolls.

_____ _____ 18. Benton opposed slavery because the institution allowed the great planters of the South to dominate the small self-supporting farmers.

_____ _____ 19. Each census revealed that the balance of political power was shifting to the West as the trans-Appalachian population grew.

_____ _____ 20. In the end, the American economy was integrated less by congressional legislation than by a revolution in transportation that conquered seasons, leveled mountains, and diverted the course of rivers.

ANSWERS

I. True–False

1. False
2. True
3. True
4. False
5. False
6. False
7. True
8. True
9. True
10. False

II. Multiple Choice

1. a
2. d
3. b
4. c
5. c
6. a
7. c

III. Quantification

VI	1.	25
LI	2.	4,000
VI	3.	90
VI	4.	6,000; double
VI	5.	7; 8
LI	6.	6; 5
VI	7.	7
LI	8.	3; 4
VI	9.	80; 1.25

VI. Fact–Judgment–Importance

1.	F	VI
2.	F	LI
3.	J	VI
4.	J	LI
5.	J	VI
6.	J	VI
7	J	VI
8.	J	LI
9.	J	VI
10.	F	VI
11.	J	LI
12.	J	VI
13.	J	VI
14.	F	VI
15.	F	LI
16.	F	VI
17.	J	VI
18.	J	VI
19.	F	VI
20.	J	VI

⊰14⊱

A Nation Awakening

Political, Diplomatic, and Economic Developments, 1815–1824

"The 'Lowell girls' lived in company-run dormitories, were watched closely, and were disciplined without ceremony for moral lapses."

"It is the true office of history to represent the events themselves, together with the counsels, and to leave the observations and conclusions thereupon to the liberty and faculty of everyman's judgment."

Bacon

I. True–False
If the statement is false, change any words necessary to make it true.

_____ 1. Washington's wife, Martha, originated the tale of George and the cherry tree.

_____ 2. In the Rush-Bagot Agreement of 1817, the United States and Britain agreed to increase warships on the Great Lakes but maintain an equal number.

_____ 3. Although the Western hemisphere was closed to further colonization, according to the Monroe Doctrine, the United States retained the right to intervene in European affairs.

_____ 4. Clothmaking was largely woman's work done in spare time by half the population.

_____ 5. The British were willing to sell their textile machinery or plans for machinery to other nations but for a very high price.

_____ 6. Because of immigration in the early 1800s, labor was abundant and wages were relatively low in North America.

_____ 7. The United States was unique among nations in raising the inventor to the status of hero.

_____ 8. Banks issued more money in paper certificates than they actually had on hand in gold and silver.

_____ 9. The first American industrial workers were boys under the age of sixteen.

_____ 10. Slaveowners in Virginia and Maryland refused, for humanitarian reasons, to sell their surplus slaves in the deep South.

II. Multiple Choice

_____ 1. The Missouri Compromise provided for all but which of the following:

   a. Missouri was admitted as a slave state
   b. Slavery was disallowed north of the southern boundary of Missouri
   c. future Missouri territory states would decide whether or not they wanted slavery
   d. Maine was admitted as a free state

_____ 2. Entertainment and recreation on the frontier was provided by all but which of the following:

   a. barn or cabin raising
   b. drinking contests
   c. husking corn contests
   d. splitting logs into rails

_____ 3. The Lowell Mills and dormitory system

   a. had a work week of 55 hours
   b. did not care much for the workers' lives away from work
   c. required workers to attend church
   d. included room and board as part of the pay

_____ 4. The industrial revolution began in which industry?

   a. textile
   b. farm machinery
   c. iron and steel
   d. steam transportation

_____ 5. John Marshall and the Supreme Court in *McCullouch v. Maryland* established that

   a. if the goal was legitimate, Congress had power to enact whatever legislation it chose
   b. the Court could reverse a state court
   c. the Court could declare a federal law unconstitutional
   d. private contracts were legal

_____ 6. The son of a prominent politician who switched from the party of his father and became a Democratic-Republican was

   a. George Jefferson
   b. Thomas Monroe
   c. Aaron Burr, Jr.
   d. John Quincy Adams

_____ 7. The Monroe Doctrine was successful because it was supported by

   a. the French army
   b. the British navy
   c. the Organization of American States
   d. the Latin-American political leaders

III. Quantification

Fill in each blank in the following statements with the correct number or numbers. Then determine whether you consider the statement to be very important (VI) or less important (LI). Write your choice in the blank to the left of each statement.

VI–LI

_____ 1. In 1821 there were _____ Federalists and _____ Democratic-Republicans in Congress.

_____ 2. In 1820 only _____ of 24 states chose presidential electors by statewide popular vote.

_____ 3. In the early nineteenth century an American carpenter made about _____ times as much money as his European counterpart.

_____ 4. Eli Whitney's dramatic show of interchangeable parts won him a government contract to make _____ more rifles.

_____ 5. In 1800 there were 290 cotton spindles in mills in New England, but in 1815 there were _____ spindles.

_____ 6. In 1820 about half the factory workers in mills were under _____ years of age.

_____ 7. In 1820 almost _____ percent of the population of Mississippi was black and in bondage.

_____ 8. Parson Weem's "biography" of Washington ran through _____ large editions from 1800 to 1820.

_____ 9. In 1820, the returns from Richmond, Virginia, a city of 12,000 people, showed that only _____ men bothered to vote.

IV. Concepts–Ideas

Identify each of the following key words briefly and explain the relationship between them and the words that follow in parentheses.

1. political stability (one party — indifference — state legislatures — voting — unopposed)

_____

_____

2. unfortified boundary (armed vessels — 49° — equal rights — concession)

_____

_____

3. Patriotism (needlepoint — Yankee Doodle — Weems — demigods — eagles and arrows — chosen people)

_____

_____

4. primacy of national government (reverse state court — unconstitutional — states subordinant — power to enact)

_____

_____

5. "essentially different" (destiny — intervene — colonization — appendage — seconded)

_____

_____

6. textile manufacturing (woman's work — spare time — tedious — natural fibers — expensive)

_____

_____

7. "cottage industry" (fiber merchant — by piece — farm women — agrarian rhythms)

_____

_____

8. power (river — steam — one roof — geared — proletriat — system — continual run)

_____

_____

9. factory (mills — workers nearby — machines — power — faster)

_____

_____

10. ingenuity (continuous operation — interchangeable parts — mechanical aptitude — everything new)

_____

_____

11. capital (merchants and shippers — banks — paper certificates — belief energy)

_____

_____

12. industrial worker (proletariat — whole families — Lowell girls — farm hours — regulated — young — idyllic)

_____

_____

13. compromise (eleven — immoral — Missouri/Maine — 36° 30' — firebell)

_____

_____

V. Essay Questions

Write notes under each of the following questions that would help you answer similar essay questions on an exam.

1. Describe the three important Supreme Court decisions of the period from 1810 to 1820 and explain which you consider most important and why.

   _____

   _____

   _____

2. What are the main features of the Monroe Doctrine? Are elements of it still "valid" today? Why or why not?

   _____

   _____

   _____

3. Explain the political situation existing in the era of good feelings. Is this stability preferable, in a democracy, to a two-party system? Why or why not?

   _____

   _____

   _____

4. In what ways was the United States ideally suited for an industrial revolution? Be specific.

   _____

   _____

   _____

5. Was the creation of a class of workers who did nothing but tend machines a beneficial change in an economic system? Explain.

   _____

   _____

   _____

6. List and explain the main inventions and innovations that brought about rapid industrial change.

   _____

   _____

   _____

7. Evaluate the labor organization of the Lowell Mills at Waltham. Was it beneficial or harmful? Why?

   _____

   _____

   _____

8. Describe the decline and revival of slavery. Is it a black mark on American history that the moral arguments against slavery yielded to the profits of cotton? Explain.

_____

_____

_____

9. Explain the Missouri Compromise. Is it good that the slavery issue was settled in 1820 for the next 40 years or would it have been preferable to face the issue "head-on" in 1820? Explain.

_____

_____

_____

10. Political, legal, economic, social, and diplomatic developments are described in the chapter (politics, Supreme Court decisions, industrial change, slavery, and relations with Europe). Which area had the most significant impact on American history in the long run? Give arguments and evidence to support your choice.

_____

_____

_____

VI. Determining Importance

For each of the following statements determine whether you consider the statement to be very important (VI) to understanding this period of history or less important (LI). Then decide whether you believe the statement is verifiable (V) or unverifiable (U). Verifiable means that evidence can be gathered to prove the statement accurate beyond a reasonable doubt. Write your choices in the blanks at the left of each statement.

VI–LI   V–U

_____   _____   1. Americans believed they were a new chosen people, unique and blessed on the face of the earth, committed to liberty, democracy, and progress.

_____   _____   2. Monroe was very successful as president, calmly meeting and promptly dispatching every problem that rose to face him.

_____   _____   3. In 1816, William Crawford had more political support than Monroe but did not take the trouble to ensure that his supporters showed up at the party caucus.

_____   _____   4. Monroe agreed with Jefferson that the government that governs least governs best.

_____   _____   5. After the Bush-Bagot and subsequent treaties, the United States and Canada shared the world's longest unfortified international boundary.

_____   _____   6. The American threat in the Monroe Doctrine forced Austria and France to abandon the project intended to help Spain regain her American colonies.

_____   _____   7. In the McCulloch decision the Supreme Court established the rights of the national government over state authority.

VI–LI   V–U

_____ _____ 8. The consequences of machines that make goods quickly and cheaply changed the terms of human existence far more profoundly than did any battle or the beheading of any king or queen.

_____ _____ 9. Industrialization created a class of workers that did nothing but tend machines.

_____ _____ 10. The English made it illegal to export machinery, to reveal their specifications, or for machine experts to leave the country.

_____ _____ 11. The labor shortage was the reason Americans were infatuated with the machine.

_____ _____ 12. In 1814 Harvard College instituted a course called "Elements of Technology," and in 1825 a college devoted to technology was founded in Troy, New York.

_____ _____ 13. As long as confidence and optimism were in rich supply, banks were a source of energy as powerful as the 32-foot falls of the Merrimack River.

_____ _____ 14. The long workweek put no one off in the early nineteenth century; it was a normal schedule for a farm family.

_____ _____ 15. There would have been a gradual, peaceful disappearance of slavery had it not been for Eli Whitney's cotton gin.

_____ _____ 16. Several northern Congressmen condemned slavery as immoral, "a sin which sits heavily on the soul of every one of us."

ANSWERS

I. True–False	II. Multiple Choice	III. Quantification		VI. Determining Importance		
1. False	1. c	1.	28; 158	1.	VI	U
2. False	2. b	2.	7	2.	LI	U
3. False	3. c	3.	3	3.	VI	V
4. True	4. a	4.	10,000	4.	VI	V
5. False	5. a	5.	130,000	5.	VI	V
6. False	6. d	6.	16	6.	LI	U
7. True	7. b	7.	50	7.	VI	V
8. True		8.	59	8.	VI	U
9. False		9.	17	9.	VI	V
10. False				10.	LI	V
				11.	LI	U
				12.	VI	V
				13.	VI	U
				14.	VI	U
				15.	LI	U
				16.	LI	V

113

=15=

Hero of the People

Andrew Jackson
and a New Era,
1824–1830

"Standing on your own two feet"
"to the victor belong the spoils"

"General tendencies do not decide alone; great personalities are always necessary to make them effective."

von Ranke

I. True–False
If the statement is false, change any words necessary to make it true.

_____ 1. In some ways public discussion was as candid and eloquent with a one-party system during the Monroe administration as before or since.

_____ 2. Jefferson and Monroe favored William H. Crawford of Georgia in the 1824 election because he favored slavery and its preservation.

_____ 3. Jackson's political views in 1824 were a mystery.

_____ 4. Jackson favored banks and paper money as a means to rapid expansion of the West.

_____ 5. Because he spent much of his life abroad, Adams did not have a circle of political associates around him.

_____ 6. The leaders of Jackson's party of the people came from the same privileged class as the group around John Quincy Adams.

_____ 7. During the 1820s and 1830s politics ceased to be the exclusive concern of the leisured classes and came to preoccupy much of the white male population.

_____ 8. Fearful of losing power to the west, the eastern states began to tighten voter qualifications in 1828 and reduce the number of eligible voters.

_____ 9. George Washington and other Founding Fathers had been members of the skeptical, free-thinking Society of Freemasons.

_____ 10. Andrew Jackson was a gracious, courtly gentleman whose public manners were the equal of royalty's.

_____ 11. Jackson was very indulgent toward children and wanted them to stand on their own two feet.

_____ 12. Original agreements had given Indians land east of the Mississippi "as long as the water runs and the grass grows."

II. Multiple Choice

_____ 1. The one factor that separated Andrew Jackson from the other candidates in the 1824 election was that

   a. he looked presidential
   b. he had fought duels
   c. he was a military hero
   d. he was from the West

_____ 2. Which of the following was *not* a characteristic of Jackson in 1824:

   a. land speculator
   b. middle class in wealth
   c. slaveowner
   d. planter

_____ 3. Jackson proposed in his first address to Congress in 1829 that all but which of the following be done:

   a. the electoral college be abolished
   b. a majority of electoral votes be needed to win
   c. the president be restricted to one term
   d. that presidents be chosen by popular vote alone

_____ 4. Jackson's new Democratic-Republican party (later the Democratic party) was made up of all but which of the following sections:

   a. Pennsylvania
   b. New York
   c. South
   d. West

_____ 5. Dorr's Rebellion was

   a. an armed uprising in Rhode Island to extend voting rights
   b. a movement to establish labor unions in Pennsylvania
   c. an attack on the Masons
   d. a movement against Clay and for Jackson in Kentucky and Tennessee

_____ 6. Which of the following was *not* a reform called for by the workingmen's parties:

   a. abolition of imprisonment for debt
   b. female equality
   c. protection of workers' tools
   d. free public education

_____ 7. The insult that stung Jackson most in the 1828 campaign was that

   a. he hanged two British subjects
   b. he killed men in a duel
   c. he had soldiers shot in military campaigns
   d. he and his wife were adulterers

_____ 8. Jackson's attitude toward women included all but which of the following:

   a. women lived in a different "sphere" than men
   b. women were inferior in morality
   c. men should show chivalry toward women
   d. women must be sheltered

_____ 9. The Indian group that developed intensive agriculture, had black slaves, printed books and newspapers, operated a school system, and developed an alphabet were the

a. Seminoles
b. Creeks
c. Iroquois
d. Cherokees

_____ 10. Jackson's reaction to the South Carolina convention's declaration that the tariff was null and void in their state was to

a. threaten to lead an army into South Carolina
b. agree in principle but protest as president
c. ignore the whole issue
d. declare a state of emergency

III. Quantification

Fill in each blank in the following statements with the correct number or numbers. Then determine the order of significance of each statistic from 1 to 7. The most important would be 1, the least important would be 7.

1–7

_____ a. _____ of the first 5 presidents were born in Virginia.

_____ b. In 1824 about _____ percent of the country's adult white males cast ballots; however, in 1840 more than _____ percent did.

_____ c. In 1832 the anti-Masonic movement elected _____ men to Congress.

_____ d. Jackson won the election of 1828 with _____ percent of the total vote, which was more than _____ times as large as the vote in 1824.

_____ e. The Trail of Tears took the Cherokee Indians _____ miles to Oklahoma, left thousands dead, and took them _____ generations to recover.

_____ f. Cotton accounted for nearly _____ of the wealth that poured into the United States from abroad.

_____ g. On one Sunday in 1839, _____ duels were fought in New Orleans.

Explain the reasons for your ranking of the two most important statistics.

a. _____

_____

_____

b. _____

_____

_____

IV. Concepts–Ideas

Identify each of the following key words briefly and explain the relationship between them and the words that follow in parentheses.

1. caucus (nominations — senators and representatives — support — accepted — State Department)

_____

_____

2. symbol (Jackson — agrarian past — hero — poor to wealth — success — riches)

_____

_____

3. "corrupt bargain" (influence in House — Secretary of State — deal — "puritan and the blackleg" — duel — revenge)

_____

_____

4. "out of tune" (not magnetic — pompous — ancestry — partisan politics — the best — aloof)

_____

_____

5. democratic rhetoric (talk politics — pleasure — people rule — time to think — extend vote — reforms — urban suffrage — popular vote)

_____

_____

6. "workies" (skilled artisans — eastern cities — debt imprisonment — lien laws — public education)

_____

_____

7. secrecy in society (free and open — business favoritism — scheme — husband and wife bond — signs — handshakes)

_____

_____

8. paranoia (periodical — diabolic — conspiracy — Jefferson — pope — anti-Semitism — irrational — anti-communism — subversives)

_____

_____

9. free society (openness — negative — laissez faire — natural laws — opportunity — artificial obstacles — self-made)

_____

_____

10. democracy and race (prejudice — Bible — nature — crushed Indians — admire — courage — regret)

_____

_____

11. spoils system (frankness — not clean sweep — not property — *any* intelligent man — own supporters— incompetent)

_____

_____

12. civilization (Cherokees — agriculture — schools — houses — newspapers — alphabet — books)

_____

_____

13. nullification (states sovereign — alliance — not enforce — two-thirds — capitulation — secession)

_____

_____

14. Code Duello (gentlemen — insult — honor — pistols — French aristocrats — New Orleans — keep score)

_____

_____

V. Essay Questions

Write notes under each of the following questions that would help you answer similar essay questions on an exam.

1. Is the caucus of senators and representatives to choose party nominations for the presidency a preferable system to conventions and primaries? Explain.

_____

_____

_____

2. Do you agree or disagree with John Quincy Adams' view that the fedceral government should take an active role in promoting economic prosperity? Explain.

_____

_____

_____

3. Describe, in some detail, the election of 1824. In what ways was it a landmark election? To what extent was it really unimportant?

_____

_____

_____

4. List and explain the beliefs and attitudes of Andrew Jackson in 1824. With which do you agree and disagree? Explain your preferences.

_____

_____

_____

5. Was the so-called "corrupt bargain" an unusual agreement in politics or a "normal democratic deal" that is part of the expected system? Explain.

_____

_____

_____

6. What were John Quincy Adams' qualities that should have made him a "great" president? What qualities were a hindrance to greatness? Should we, as a nation, have encouraged Adams' qualities over those of Jackson? Why or why not?

_____

_____

_____

7. What were the reasons for the age of the common man? Were these changes beneficial and desirable? Explain.

_____

_____

_____

8. Describe the anti-Mason movement and the paranoid streak in American politics. Is this attitude still a danger in American society? Explain.

_____

_____

_____

9. Describe the mud-slinging in the 1828 campaign. Is slinging mud inevitable in a democracy? Why or why not? Can it be controlled? Explain.

_____

_____

_____

10. What were Jackson's views about women, blacks, and Indians? Should we condemn him for these views or just acknowledge that he was a product of his time? Explain.

_____

_____

_____

11. Describe the process of Indian removal. Is this to be looked upon as sad but inevitable or as a black mark upon American society and history? Explain.

_____

_____

_____

12. Explain the principles involved in nullification. What practical problems brought the issue to the forefront? Was Jackson correct in his reaction? Explain. Do you agree or disagree with Calhoun's *The South Carolina Exposition and Protest?* Why or why not?

_____

_____

_____

VI. Determining Importance

Determine whether you consider each of the following statements to be very important (VI) or less important (LI). Then decide whether each statement can be proven by research and is verifiable (V) or probably can never really be proven in spite of research and is unverifiable (U). Write your choices in the blanks to the left of each statement.

VI–LI   V–U

_____ _____ 1. Jackson was the first chief executive to come from the West.

_____ _____ 2. In 1828, opponents of Adams made a great fuss over his purchase (he paid for it) of a billiard table because this was a game for aristocrats.

_____ _____ 3. It was the task of government to preserve freedom of opportunity by striking down artificial obstacles to improvement, such as laws that benefited only a few.

_____ _____ 4. Jackson's vision of equal opportunity, which represented the dominant opinion of the era, extended only to white males.

_____ _____ 5. Jackson admired the native Americans for their closeness to nature and their courage in resisting their conquerors.

_____ _____ 6. Jackson vetoed the Maysville Road Bill but acknowledged that if a constitutional amendment were passed to allow it, he would approve it.

_____ _____ 7. The Seminoles of Florida (allied with runaway slaves) were never defeated and held out in swamplands against the army.

_____ _____ 8. Were it not for their color the Cherokees would have been good Jacksonians, for the organization of their society conformed with his principles.

_____ _____ 9. Chief Justice Marshall ruled that George had no authority over the Cherokee territory and that the state could not force them to give up their land.

_____ _____ 10. South Carolina cotton planters believed that the high tariff meant that they were paying the whole country's bill and underwriting industrial investments.

VI–LI   V–U

_____ _____ 11.   John C. Calhoun maintained that the Union had been formed not by the people of America as a whole, but by the people acting through individual states of which they were citizens.

_____ _____ 12.   Of the southern statesmen who rose to prominence after 1790, hardly one can be mentioned who was not involved in a duel.

_____ _____ 13.   Most duels were fought over politics, not women.

_____ _____ 14.   Daniel Boorstin maintains that to the upper class in the South the unwritten laws of honor, manliness, decency, and courage were more important than the laws of legislatures.

Pick out the two statements that you consider the most important and explain why you think so.

a. _____
   _____
   _____

b. _____
   _____
   _____

Pick out one statement that you consider less important and explain why you think so.

_____
_____
_____

VII. Fact–Judgment

Determine whether you consider each of the following statements to be a fact (F) or a judgment (J). A judgment may be true and you may agree with it, but it remains a judgment because it is *derived from* a fact and not a fact itself. It could be either a reasoned judgment or a professional interpretation. Write your choice in the blank to the left of the statement.

F–J

_____ 1.   A single party could not contain the personal ambitions of every prominent politician, and there were not enough nominations to high offices to go around.

_____ 2.   John Quincy Adams believed the federal government should take an active role in promoting economic prosperity, including the financing of internal improvements.

_____ 3.   Jackson never had a real understanding of the needs of an industrial capitalist economy.

_____ 4.   No matter what his political ideas, Jackson was an embodiment of the American success story, a symbol of the American quest for riches.

121

———— 5. Stephen Van Rensselaer, who cast the deciding vote for Adams in the 1824 election, said he received guidance from on high in the form of a paper with "Adams" written on it on the floor at his feet.

———— 6. The temperamental Adams was out of touch with his time, without a magnetic personality, and standoffish.

———— 7. It was President Adams' custom to rise early, walk to the Potomac River, shed his clothes, and take a swim.

———— 8. The democratic upheaval was partially due to the fact that survival was easier and people had more time to think about public affairs.

———— 9. According to some politicians, the Masonic order was a conspiracy aimed at keeping the common man down.

———— 10. From time to time in American history, movements based on a hysterical fear of conspiracy win large numbers of votes.

———— 11. The Jackson campaign of 1828 was the "dirtiest" that the United States or any nation had ever experienced.

———— 12. The state of Georgia defied the Supreme Court and forcibly removed the Cherokees.

ANSWERS

I. True–False	II. Multiple Choice	III. Quantification	IV. Determining Importance		VII. Fact–Judgment
1. True	1. c	1. 4	1. VI	V	1. J
2. False	2. b	2. 25; 75	2. LI	V	2. F
3. True	3. d	3. 53	3. VI	U	3. J
4. False	4. a	4. 56; 3	4. VI	U	4. J
5. True	5. a	5. 1,200; 3	5. LI	V	5. F
6. True	6. b	6. half	6. VI	V	6. J
7. True	7. d	7. 10	7. LI	V	7. F
8. False	8. b		8. VI	U	8. J
9. True	9. d		9. VI	V	9. F
10. True	10. a		10. VI	U	10. J
11. True			11. VI	V	11. J
12. True			12. LI	U	12. F
			13. LI	U	
			14. VI	U	

—16—

In the Shadow of Andrew Jackson

Personalities and Politics, 1830–1842

"Our Union: It must be preserved."
"The Union, next to our liberty, the most dear."

"The historians are the guardians of tradition, the priests of the cult of natonality, the prophets of social reform, the exponents and upholders of national virtue and glory."

Bagby

I. True–False
If the statement is false, change any words necessary to make it true.

_____ 1. Although he went through physical hardship in duels, wars, and striving to succeed, Jackson was basically a healthy man.

_____ 2. Calhoun believed that the South and its institutions were threatened by northern industrial interests.

_____ 3. Jackson could not get anyone to associate with Peggy Eaton except Van Buren and his own niece.

_____ 4. At one point Calhoun favored punishing Jackson for his unauthorized invasion of Florida.

_____ 5. Biddle lent money to several Jackson supporters, but he refused to retire the national debt as Jackson wanted.

_____ 6. Clay persuaded Biddle to apply for a new bank charter in 1832 though the existing one would not have expired until 1836.

_____ 7. The few blacks allowed to vote drifted into the Whig party.

_____ 8. In 1836 the Whigs named three candidates to run against Van Buren in those parts of the country where they were most popular.

_____ 9. Harrison felt that a president should take an active part in initiating legislation and guiding it through Congress.

_____ 10. In colleges during the first half of the nineteenth century there were lists of detailed rules, curfews, required attendance at religious services, and a demand for deference to professors.

II. Multiple Choice

_____ 1. In order to force acceptance of Peggy Eaton into social circles, Jackson

   a. summoned a cabinet meeting on the subject
   b. admitted her sordid background but insisted she had reformed
   c. got the cooperation of his niece to accept her
   d. made her a receptionist at the White House

_____ 2. "Our Union: It must be preserved," was a toast made by

   a. John C. Calhoun
   b. Henry Clay
   c. Andrew Jackson
   d. Daniel Webster

_____ 3. Biddle's Bank of the United States was able to destroy any other bank because

   a. of the size of its deposits
   b. it told other banks what interest rates to charge
   c. it had more paper money of state banks than they had specie
   d. it had government funds available

_____ 4. The Bank of the United States had as supporters

   a. freewheeling bankers of the West
   b. conservative hard-money people
   c. New York "Wall Street" bankers
   d. none of the above

_____ 5. Which of the following was _not_ true about Daniel Webster?

   a. He was an alcoholic
   b. He invested money foolishly
   c. He favored states' rights for New England
   d. He received money from New England industrialists

_____ 6. In 1840, the charge against Harrison that backfired on the Democrats was that he

   a. was an Indian fighter
   b. was born in a log cabin and drank cider
   c. was an effeminate fop
   d. would be happy with a pension of $2,000

_____ 7. A "liberal" education in the 1830s meant

   a. education suitable to a free man
   b. really a conservative education
   c. one that agreed with the Bill of Rights
   d. none of the above

III. Quantification

Fill in each blank in the following statements with the correct number or numbers. Then determine whether you consider the statement to be very important (VI) or less important (LI). Write your choice in the blank to the left of each statement.

VI–LI

_____ 1. The Bank of the United States had _____ branches, controlled _____ of all bank deposits, and did $ _____ million in transactions each year.

_____ 2. In the election of 1832, after vetoing the bank bill, Jackson won _____ percent of the popular vote and _____ electoral votes to Clay's _____ .

_____ 3. Many of the _____ "pet banks" into which Jackson had placed federal money were irresponsible in using the money.

_____ 4. In 1836, Clay convinced Congress to distribute $ _____ million to the states for expenditure on internal improvements.

_____ 5. The patchwork alliance of the Whig party won _____ seats in the House of Representatives in 1834 and almost _____ the Senate.

_____ 6. Van Buren gained _____ percent of the vote in the 1840 election but lost in the electoral college 60 to _____ .

_____ 7. In 1860, only _____ of the 246 colleges and universities were state institutions.

_____ 8. The Preemption Act of 1841 provided that a family that had "squatted" on up to _____ acres of public land could purchase it at the minimum price of $ _____ per acre.

IV. Concepts–Ideas

Identify each of the following key words briefly and explain the relationship between them and the words that follow in parentheses.

1. southern institutions (slavery — plantation — aristocracy — state sovereignty — obsession)

_____

_____

2. snobbery (sailor's wife — marriage — cabinet — snubbed — moralistic — niece — command)

_____

_____

3. central bank (vaults — bonds — deposits — payments — branches — control — borrow)

_____

_____

4. symbol (changed politics — initiative — veto — democratic upheaval — passions — embodiment)

_____

_____

5. Whig (veto — Indians — Bank — education and means — American system — high tariff — anti-Masons)

_____

_____

6. panic (no specie — factories — bankruptcy — default — subtreasury — laissez-faire)

_____

_____

7. log cabin (hard cider — incompetent — slip — snobbery — humble — simple — elitists — democracy)

_____

_____

8. curriculum (ancient languages — liberal — literature — science — philosophy — no electives — prescribed)

_____

_____

9. deference (curfew — rules — religious services — politeness — professors — taunted — defied — mobs — conformity)

_____

_____

10. boundary settlement (U.S./Canada) — port wine — forged — Mesabi Range — settlement — compromise — generous)

_____

_____

_____

V. Essay Questions

Write notes under each of the following questions that would help you answer similar essay questions on an exam.

1. Explain the Peggy Eaton Affair. Should a president be above this kind of soap opera affair or are all presidents and their wives subject to this type of social tangle? Explain.

_____

_____

2. Point out the pros and cons of the Bank of the United States. Would you have approved the bank or opposed it? Why?

_____

_____

_____

3. Trace the financial development of the United States from Jackson's veto of the bank recharter in 1832 to the depression of 1837. Was the end of the national bank a cause of the depression? Why or why not?

_____

_____

_____

4. Who were the enemies of the Bank and what were the reasons for their opposition?

_____

_____

_____

5. What were the similarities and differences in the elections of 1836 and 1840?

_____

_____

_____

6. Who would have made the best president in the period from 1837 to 1845—Van Burren, Clay, Harrison, Tyler, or Webster? Give evidence to support your choice.

_____

_____

_____

7. Was the "style" of elections in 1828, 1832, 1836, and 1840 evidence of the final arrival of democracy—decisions made by the common man—or was it the beginning of images and personalities over issues? Explain.

_____

_____

_____

8. Describe college life in the first half of the nineteenth century. What do you see as worthwhile and what do you note to be undesirable? Be specific.

_____

_____

_____

9. What were the issues and conditions of settlement of the Webster-Ashburton Treaty? Why was the United States able to settle differences with England by negotiation and yet used force or the threat of force with Spain, the Indians, and later, Mexico?

_____

_____

_____

10. Should Andrew Jackson be considered a great president, in the top six or seven in our history? Why or why not?

_____

_____

_____

VI. Determining Importance–Verifiable–Unverifiable

Determine whether you consider each of the following statements to be very important (VI) or less important (LI). Then decide whether each statement can be proven by research and is verifiable (V) or probably can never really be proven in spite of research and is unverifiable (U). Write your choices in the blanks to the left of each statement.

VI–LI   V–U

_____ _____ 1. Jackson suffered from lead poisoning, headaches, diarrhea, coughing fits, kidney disease, and edema. He also suffered two serious hemorrhages of the lungs.

_____ _____ 2. The leader of the snubbers of Peggy Eaton appeared to be Florida Calhoun, as sternly moralistic a Presbyterian as her husband.

_____ _____ 3. Van Buren, an old hand at charm and chitchat, was gracious and witty.

_____ _____ 4. In the challenge of toasts at a dinner party, Jackson took satisfaction that Calhoun trembled as he spoke the last toast on liberty over union.

_____ _____ 5. The policies of the B.U.S. remained in the hands of individuals who were responsible not to the people but to the shareholders.

_____ _____ 6. In July 1836, Jackson issued the Specie Circular, which required that government lands be paid for in gold and silver coin, not paper money.

_____ _____ 7. Jackson was not a wise man. His intelligence was limited, his education spotty, and he was easily ruled by his passions.

_____ _____ 8. Webster was influential more for his presence and his peerless oratorical powers (his eyes burned like "anthracite furnaces") than for any of his political stances.

_____ _____ 9. Webster came to expect money in the mail after every speech on behalf of the tariff or even the ideal of the Union.

_____ _____ 10. Van Buren, after the depression began, attempted to separate the government from the banks by keeping government funds in its own vaults.

_____ _____ 11. Harrison delivered a turgid treatise on Roman history that still stands as the longest inauguration speech ever given.

_____ _____ 12. Harrison died of pneumonia that developed from a cold caught at the wet and windy Inauguration on April 4, 1841, exactly one month after taking office.

VII. Fact–Judgment–Importance

Determine whether you consider each of the following statements to be a fact (F) or a judgment (J). A judgment may be true and you may agree with it, but it remains a judgment because it is *derived from* fact and not a fact itself. It could be either a reasoned judgment or a professional interpretation. Then decide whether each statement is very important (VI) or less important (LI). Write your choices in the blanks to the left of the statement.

F–J   VI–LI

_____ _____ 1. Calhoun was possessed of the keen, logical mind that the impulsive and emotional Jackson lacked.

_____ _____ 2. The Peggy Eaton affair illustrates how the direction of history can turn on trivial incidents.

_____ _____ 3. No one was more important than Van Buren in constructing the Democratic machine and ensuring votes in the future by rewarding supporters with government jobs.

_____ _____ 4. Nicholas Biddle told Congressmen that the B.U.S. was capable of destroying any other bank in the country.

_____ _____ 5. The New York City "Wall Street" bankers and brokers resented the Philadelphia financier's (Biddle's) exercise of the ultimate money power.

_____ _____ 6. The working class of the Democratic party lumped Biddle along with some of the unscrupulous banks and inveigled against his monopolistic powers.

_____ _____ 7. Locofocos got their name from the self-igniting matches they used when the Democrats turned off the gas lights at one of their meetings.

_____ _____ 8. Webster declared that the Constitution was the wellspring of American liberty, and the indissoluble union of the states, its greatest defense.

_____ _____ 9. Clay's strength was also his weakness: he had taken too many strong stands on issues and, in doing so, made too many enemies.

_____ _____ 10. In the campaign of 1840, Whigs depicted Van Buren as an effeminate fop who sipped champagne, ate fancy French food, perfumed his whiskers, and flitted about in silks and satins.

_____ _____ 11. After the campaign and election of 1840, never again in the egalitarian United States would there be political profit in appealing to the superior qualifications of "the better sort."

_____ _____ 12. When Tyler vetoed one bank bill after another, the Whig majority expelled the president from the party, and Tyler's cabinet resigned.

_____ _____ 13. When a group of blacks on the brig *Creole* mutinied, killed the crew, and sailed to the British Bahamas, the British hanged the leaders of the mutiny but freed the other slaves.

_____ _____ 14. In the negotiations with Webster over the Canadian-American border, Lord Ashburton gave to the United States the Mesabi Range area, one of the world's richest iron-ore deposits.

_____ _____ 15. By 1850, some universities had established medical and law schools but apprenticeships were still the most common means of preparing for those professions.

VIII. Chronology

Number the following events in their correct chronological order from 1 to 10.

1–10

_____ a. Webster-Ashburton Treaty

_____ b. census report showing New York with 349,000 population

_____ c. Oberlin College admits women students

_____ d. most serious time of the depression

_____ e. Jackson's election to a second term

_____ f. founding of Mount Holyoke College for women

_____ g. application by Biddle for a new bank charter

_____ h. death of William Henry Harrison

_____ i. the Jackson-Calhoun toasts on Union and Liberty

_____ j. Webster's speech in Congress on the importance of the Constitution and Union

ANSWERS

I. True–False

1. False
2. True
3. False
4. True
5. False
6. True
7. True
8. True
9. False
10. True

II. Multiple Choice

1. a
2. c
3. c
4. d
5. c
6. b
7. a

III. Quantification

VI 1. 29; one third; 70
VI 2. 55; 219; 49
VI 3. 89
VI 4. 37
LI 5. 89; half
LI 6. 47; 234
LI 7. 17
VI 8. 160; 1.25

VI. Determining Importance–Verifiable–Unverifiable

1.	LI	V
2.	VI	U
3.	LI	U
4.	LI	U
5.	VI	V
6.	VI	V
7.	LI	U
8.	LI	U
9.	LI	U
10.	VI	V
11.	LI	U
12.	LI	V

VII. Fact–Judgment–Importance

1.	J	VI
2.	J	VI
3.	J	VI
4.	F	VI
5.	J	VI
6.	J	VI
7.	F	LI
8.	F	VI
9.	J	VI
10.	J	LI
11.	J	VI
12.	F	LI
13.	F	LI
14.	F	VI
15.	F	LI

VIII. Chronology

a.	10
b.	8
c.	5
d.	9
e.	4
f.	6
g.	3
h.	7
i.	1
j.	2

17

A Culture in Ferment

Sects, Utopias, and Visionaries

The American way of life "throws him back forever upon himself alone, and threatens in the end to confine him entirely within the solitude of his own heart."

Tocqueville

"We get our ethics from our history and judge our history by our ethics."

Troeltsch

I.   True–False
If the statement is false, change any words necessary to make it true.

_____ 1.   Tocqueville saw in Americans a love of the new and contempt for the old and the relentless pursuit of money.

_____ 2.   The Congregationalists had supported the war for independence and supported Thomas Jefferson in the 1790s.

_____ 3.   Many Americans went to camp meetings for the show and the chance to steal, heckle preachers, drink, and philander.

_____ 4.   Many religious leaders originated in "the burned-over district" in New York State, an area of immense forest fires.

_____ 5.   The *Book of Mormon* was a Bible of the New World that told about a lost tribe of Israel in America, the Nephites.

_____ 6.   The Shakers believed that Christ would return to earth at any time; therefore, there was no need to perpetuate the human race.

_____ 7.   Robert Owen, a British industrialist, believed that only a communal style of living would overcome the innate evil in human beings.

_____ 8. One member of the Fruitlands community lived one year on nothing but crackers and the next on apples.

_____ 9. To Europeans, transcendentalism meant to go beyond the spiritual world to pure reason and reliance on the material world.

_____ 10. For most Americans of the early nineteenth century, pork was more common on their tables than beef.

Multiple Choice

_____ 1. Which of the following was *not* a feature of transcendentalism?

   a. nature over civilization
   b. personal morality over laws
   c. an insistence on consistency
   d. the capacity within oneself to be happy

_____ 2. The utopian community which practiced "free love" was the

   a. Oneida
   b. Fruitland
   c. New Harmony
   d. Icarians

_____ 3. The reason Brigham Young was frustrated with the American victory over Mexico was

   a. he had helped support the Mexicans
   b. it brought the Mormons back under the American flag
   c. Utah had been granted independence by the Mexican government
   d. several American leaders had promised to end Mormonism after defeating the Mexicans

_____ 4. The revivalist sermon normally began with

   a. a note of hope for salvation
   b. a gruesome, detailed description of hell
   c. a statement on the need for support offerings
   d. an emotional description of the sinfulness of humans

_____ 5. Converts flocked to join William Miller's Adventists group when

   a. he advocated "free love"
   b. he introduced a complex mathematical formula
   c. a magnificent comet appeared in the sky for a month
   d. he published a newspaper and predicted the day of the end of the world

_____ 6. The publication of *Alhambra* established what American writer in the English literary establishment?

   a. Henry David Thoreau
   b. Washington Irving
   c. Bret Harte
   d. Samuel Clemens

_____ 7. The author who made guilt, sin, and moral decay his or her themes was

   a. Margaret Fuller
   b. Franklin Pierce
   c. Nathaniel Hawthorne
   d. Oliver Wendell Holmes

III. Quantification

Fill in each blank in the following statements with the correct number or numbers. Then determine whether you consider the statement to be very important (VI) or less important (LI). Write your choice in the blank to the left of each statement.

VI–LI

_____ 1. Before 1828 about _____ books about the United States were published in Europe; _____ were published in the 1830s.

_____ 2. Brigham Young had _____ wives and _____ children.

_____ 3. During the 1830s, the Shakers maintained more than _____ neat and comfortable communities in the eastern and midwestern states.

_____ 4. As many as _____ preachers simultaneously harangued the crowds in camp meetings.

_____ 5. In some cases up to _____ would attend a camp meeting coming from as far as _____ miles.

IV. Concepts–Ideas

Identify each of the following key words briefly and explain the relationship between them and the words that follow in parentheses.

1. on the move (the new — alone — solitude — house on rollers — trotted — instability — whittle — displaced)

_____

_____

2. materialism (pursuit of money — dollar — financial cycle — debtor — impoverished)

_____

_____

3. awakening (tainted — democratic — everyone — sin — hell — hope — rural — revival)

_____

_____

4. camp meetings (forest — electrifying — stumps — continuous — moans — passionate — "jerks")

_____

_____

5. circuit rider (settlements — marriage — baptism — theological differences — Methodists — denominations — survived)

_____

_____

6. Adventism (Second Coming — sermons — mathematical formula — comet — sell possessions — hills — soon — Saturday)

_____

_____

7. special revelation (Joseph Smith — gold plates — inscriptions — Nephites — prophet — Christ in America — priesthood — Gentiles)

_____

_____

8. utopia (commune — celibacy — social aspects — goodness of man — freeloaders — lazy — "impractical" — complex marriage)

_____

_____

9. transcendentalism (feelings — nature — personal morality — within oneself — beyond the material — "oversoul" — force — optimism)

_____

_____

10. "complex marriage" (property — miserable — every man, every woman — eugenics — superior have children — continence)

_____

_____

V. Essay Questions

Write notes under each of the following questions that would help you answer similar essay questions on an exam.

1. List the observations and judgments about American society made by Alex de Tocqueville and Frances Trollope. Which of these do you believe to be accurate and which not to be true? Explain why.

_____

_____

2. Is it beneficial to have a society in constant movement—geographically and socially? Why or why not?

_____

_____

3. Write an essay on rural religion of the period—revivalists, camp meetings, and circuit riders. Speculate as to what impact all of this religious enthusiasm and upheaval may have had on American society and the American mind.

_____

_____

4. Who were the Adventists? How can you explain their continued success after their leader's prediction failed?

_____

_____

5. Trace the Mormon movement from its beginning to its establishment at Salt Lake City. Would you consider the Mormons another Christian denomination or a new religion? Explain.

_____

_____

6. Write an essay on utopian communities in the first half of the nineteenth century. Include the Rappites, Shakers, Robert Owen's groups, Fruitlands, and Oneida. What were the similarities shared by these groups? Why have they never had large-scale success in America?

_____

_____

7. Explain transcendentalism. Do you believe it to be a profound philosophy with deep insights or, as Herman Melville termed it, "gibberish?" Explain your view.

_____

_____

8. Why are some of the impressions given by Thoreau about his experiences in the "wilderness" not exactly accurate?

_____

_____

9. Compare the literary contributions of Nathaniel Hawthorne and Margaret Fuller to that of Emerson and Thoreau. Which of the two groups impress you the most? Why?

_____

_____

10. Write an essay on the importance of pork in American society in the early nineteenth century.

_____

_____

_____

VI. Fact–Judgment–Relevance

Determine whether you consider each of the following statements to be a fact (F) or a judgment (J). A judgment may be true and you may agree with it, but it remains a judgment because it is _derived from_ fact and not a fact itself. It could be either a reasoned judgment or a professional interpretation. Then decide whether you believe the statement to be very relevant (VR) or less relevant (LR) to an understanding of the ideas in ferment in the period. Write your choices in the blanks to the left of the statement.

F–J   VR–LR

_____ _____   1. Before the 1820s literate Europeans thought of the United States as a remote, semi-civilized, uncultured backwater.

_____ _____   2. Tocqueville stated that in America "every man forgets his ancestors" which "threatens in the end to confine him entirely within the solitude of his own heart."

_____ _____   3. The topsy-turvy boom and bust financial cycle turned rich men into debtors overnight and threw workers out of jobs that had barely kept their families fed.

_____ _____   4. The educated middle and upper classes abandoned Calvinism because its doctrines did not agree with the benign world they saw around them.

_____ _____   5. Unlike the Puritans, Finney said that everyone who repented and prayed for deliverance would be blessed, not just a few "Elect."

_____ _____   6. Europeans listed the camp meeting as one of the two sights (a slave auction was the other) they insisted on seeing in America.

_____ _____   7. Laying out a neat city with irrigation ditches and broad avenues, the Mormons made the desert bloom.

_____ _____   8. Nineteenth-century advocates of communal living insisted that private property was a gross evil because it set people in competition with one another.

_____ _____   9. Although both the Rappites and the Shakers practiced celibacy, the Shakers lasted longer because they sought converts and adopted orphans.

_____ _____   10. Robert Owen believed in the goodness of human nature, was incapable of throwing out the freeloaders, and returned to Scotland in 1827, disillusioned and a good deal poorer.

_____ _____   11. Emerson claimed that "consistency is the hobgoblin of little minds" and that the truly enlightened human being could dispose "very easily of the most disagreeable facts."

_____ _____   12. Thoreau often took the walk from Walden Pond to Concord when he neded a decent meal or keg of nails.

_____ _____   13. When Hawthorne looked into the human heart, he saw evil rather than Emerson's divinity.

_____ _____ 14. In an 1837 address at Harvard, Emerson called for a declaration of independence from European literary themes and styles.

_____ _____ 15. Noyes believed that marriage was itself a form of property because the husband effectively owned his wife, a circumstance that made them both miserable, so he devised the concept of "complex marriage."

VII. Matching

Match the following writers with their ideas, subjects, or style of writing.

_____ 1. James Fenimore Cooper	a.	tales based on old Dutch folklore of the Hudson Valley
_____ 2. Herman Melville	b.	mystery stories with deep meaning
_____ 3. Washington Irving	c.	wrote about the meeting of the frontier and civilization
_____ 4. Margaret Fuller	d.	political radical, activist, devoted to social action
_____ 5. Nathaniel Hawthorne	e.	writer of essays on the oversoul and self-reliance
_____ 6. Edgar Allen Poe	f.	themes of guilt, sin, and moral decay
_____ 7. Henry Wadsworth Longfellow	g.	study of evil against the backdrop of a whaling voyage
_____ 8. Ralph Waldo Emerson	h.	verses on homey themes and long narrative poems
	i.	wrote about his experiences close to nature

ANSWSERS

I. True–False	II. Multiple Choice	III. Quantification	VI. Fact–Judgment–Relevance		VII. Matching
1. True	1. c	VI 1. 40; hundreds	1.	J VR	1. c
2. False	2. a	LI 2. 27; 56	2.	J LR	2. g
3. True	3. b	VI 3. 20	3.	F VR	3. a
4. False	4. d	LI 4. 40	4.	J VR	4. d
5. True	5. c	VI 5. 20,000; 200	5.	F LR	5. f
6. True	6. b		6.	F LR	6. b
7. False	7. c		7.	F VR	7. h
8. True			8.	F VR	8. e
9. False			9.	F LR	
10. True			10.	J VR	
			11.	F LR	
			12.	F VR	
			13.	J VR	
			14.	F VR	
			15.	F LR	

⊹⊱18⊰⊹

Heyday of Reform

Fighting Evil, Battling Social Problems

"I know nothing"
"going on the wagon"

"There is a tide in the affairs of men, which, taken at the flood, leads to fortune."

Shakespeare

I. True–False
    If the statement is false, change any words necessary to make it true.

_____ 1. The most important of the evangelical reform movements dealt with slavery and with women's rights.

_____ 2. Thomas Gallander arrived at his technique to help the deaf by working with cotton in his ears.

_____ 3. Dorothea Dix worked through the state legislature to achieve her reforms for the insane.

_____ 4. Because of the reform fervor, legislatures were generous in their support of penal institutions.

_____ 5. Abstainers said that alcohol was addictive and one must swear off drink completely in order to live morally.

_____ 6. Women complained about much in marriage but not about the man's control over property of the family.

_____ 7. The Order of the Star-Spangled Banner was a secret organization dedicated to shutting off further immigration.

_____ 8. The custom of drinking was too strong to be abolished by ordinances, and the prohibition laws were flagrantly ignored.

_____ 9. One effort at reform for women was to end the use of the corset and replace it with a loose bodice and ankle-length pantaloons.

_____ 10. The majority of Americans were indifferent to the anti-Catholic movement and stood by the First Amendment guarantees of religious freedom.

II. Multiple Choice

_____ 1. The Pennsylvania System of reform called for

a. large workrooms for prisoners
b. absolutely no conversation
c. solidary confinement
d. a common dining hall

_____ 2. Americans drank a great quantity for all but which of the following reasons?

a. grains were abundant and cheap
b. social acceptance in the middle and upper classes
c. workingmen received a ration on the job
d. Dr. Rush taught that it was healthful

_____ 3. A former Whig president who ran on the American party ticket was

a. Millard Fillmore
b. William Henry Harrison
c. Henry Clay
d. Abraham Lincoln

_____ 4. "The Declaration of Sentiments and Resolutions" of the women at Seneca Falls began

a. "Be it known to all men ..."
b. "Eve came from Adam's rib, not his foot ... "
c. "When in the course of human events ... "
d. "Women are and have a right to be equal ... "

_____ 5. All four of the Founding Mothers worked with which religious group?

a. Quakers
b. Presbyterians
c. Protestant missionaries
d. Seventh-Day Adventists

_____ 6. The publisher of the temperance and women's rights newspaper _The Lily_ was

a. Susan B. Anthony
b. Neal Dow
c. Amelia Jenks Bloomer
d. Henry David Thoreau

_____ 7. Hawaiians resisted somewhat the Protestant missionary effort because it

a. clashed with their mythology
b. favored the poorer Hawaiians
c. was never in their proper language
d. demanded that they cover up their bodies

III. Quantification

Fill in each blank in the following statements with the correct number or numbers. Then determine whether you consider the statement to be very important (VI) or less important (LI). Write your choice in the blank to the left of each statement.

VI–LI

_____ 1. There were as many as _____ capital offenses in some states.

_____ 2. In 1820, there were about _____ distilleries in the United States.

_____ 3. By 1835 there were _____ temperance societies in the United States with a membership of more than _____ million people.

_____ 4. By 1860, _____ states had prohibition laws, but by 1868 they had been repealed in every state but Maine.

_____ 5. In 1820, _____ Europeans came to the United States; however, in 1850 _____ arrived here.

_____ 6. At its peak, the American party ("Know-Nothings") swept to power in many states and elected _____ congressmen.

_____ 7. By 1836 the American Tract Society claimed to have distributed _____ million publications explaining Protestant beliefs to Catholics.

_____ 8. Only _____ women and _____ men signed the Seneca Falls Declaration.

IV. Concepts–Ideas

Identify each of the following key words briefly and explain the relationship between them and the words that follow in parentheses. Then in the blanks to the left, rank the five most important concepts for understanding the chapter topic from 1 to 5.

1–5

_____ 1. rejection of false idols (withdrew — closed communities — leave — get out — tolerate — next life — above it)

_____

_____

_____ 2. to do good (reform — light candle — moral duty — uplifting — neglected — disadvantage — Christian)

_____

_____

_____ 3. publicize techniques (not a commodity — trade secret — demonstrated — encourages — showmen — share)

_____

_____

_____ 4. insanity (families — legal authorities — prison — asylum — admission — antics — inhumane)

_____

_____ 5. punishment (not prison — hanging — flogging — ears, cheeks — stocks — appropriation of funds)

_____

_____ 6. correction (schools of criminality — punish — protect — solitary confinement — meditate — workrooms — silence — economical)

_____

_____ 7. social ridicule (stocks — helpless — awkward — jesting — dunce caps)

_____

_____ 8. drinking alcohol (grains cheap — everyday — workingmen — social — drunkenness — temperance — crime — poverty)

_____

_____ 9. prohibition (temperance — abstinence — law — persuasion — morality — divided — poor — evangelical — reformers)

_____

_____ 10. anti-Catholicism (Irish — German — Papal States — antidemocratic — pay rate — mobs — "Know-Nothings")

_____

_____ 11. foreign missions (Catholics — Jews — responsibility — idle educated young — Hawaii — manners — surplus women

_____

_____ 12. women's equality (Seneca Falls — vote — property — behavior — professions — most against — abolitionism)

_____

_____

V. Essay Questions

Write notes under each of the following questions that would help you answer similar essay questions on an exam.

1. Describe both attitudes toward the deaf and the blind and the activities of Gallaudet and Howe to improve their treatment.

   _____

   _____

   _____

2. Evaluate Dorothea Dix's methods of bringing about change in the treatment of the insane. Are these methods still viable today? Why or why not? What is most shocking about the treatment of the insane? Why?

   _____

   _____

   _____

3. Explain the three methods of dealing with criminals—the traditional, the Pennsylvania System, and the Auburn System. Which, in your opinion, was preferable?

   _____

   _____

   _____

4. Describe drinking habits in the United States in the early 1800s.

   _____

   _____

   _____

5. What efforts were made to reduce the consumption of alcohol in the United States? Would you support the teetotalers or the moderation, temperance reformers? Why? Would you support those who favored legislation or those who favored moral suasion? Why? Would you support none of the above groups? Why?

   _____

   _____

   _____

6. List and explain the objections to Roman Catholics in the period 1830 to 1860. In your judgment was the religious factor, the economic factor, or the cultural factor most important in the fear and antagonism of Protestants? Give evidence to support your answer.

   _____

   _____

   _____

7. What were examples of the serious discrimination against women in the United States in the period from 1800 to 1860?

_____

_____

8. Did women's rights leaders make the right decision in yielding to abolitionism as a more important reform in the 1850s? Why?

_____

_____

9. Compare and contrast the background and efforts at reform of Mott, Stanton, Bloomer, and Anthony. What important decisions did they make? In what ways do they disprove the usual image of "feminist reformers"?

_____

_____

10. Rank the following reformers according to what you consider to be their importance in techniques, impact, and consequences from 1 to 8. The most important would be 1, the least important would be 8.

1–8

_____ Susan B. Anthony   _____ Samuel Gridley Howe

_____ Neal Dow   _____ Dorothea Lynde Dix

_____ Cesare Beccaria   _____ Mott and Stanton

_____ Thomas Gallauder   _____ Amelia Jenks Bloomer

Explain your choice for the most important. Explain your choice for the least important.

_____

_____

VI. Fact–Judgment–Importance

Determine whether you consider each of the following statements to be a fact (F) or a judgment (J). A judgment may be true and you may agree with it, but it remains a judgment because it is *derived from* fact and not a fact itself. It could be either a reasoned judgment or a professional interpretation. Then determine whether you consider each statement to be very important (VI) or less important (LI). Write your choices in the blanks to the left of the statement.

F–J   VI–LI

_____   _____   1. In Jacksonian America, democracy, individualism, and the competition for riches were the dominant gods.

_____   _____   2. In the conversion experiences, converts said they would tolerate the world but reserve the pursuit of happiness for the next life.

_____   _____   3. Blindness and deafness were not considered disabilities, but conditions of life for which no one was "responsible."

_____   _____   4. Pennsylvania kept its convicts in solitary confinement so they could reflect on their crimes and not offend again.

_____   _____   5. Reformers in the 1830s rejected the ancient belief that the sight of a man being hanged provided a grim lesson for onlookers.

_____   _____   6. Unfortunately the work of those reformers interested in reforming the whole society amounted to the imposition of the moral code of a few on the many.

_____   _____   7. Urban workingmen insisted that they needed liquor for strength and laborers received a ration as part of a day's pay.

_____   _____   8. Temperance and prohibition in the beginning were originally Protestant movements supported by evangelical reformers and directed toward Protestant Americans.

_____   _____   9. Both the Irish and the Germans drank alcoholic beverages as part of their way of life, and most of the Irish and half the Germans were Roman Catholic.

_____   _____   10. The Scandinavian and German immigrants formed large communities that retained their native languages and preserved Old World customs.

_____   _____   11. Because the Irish immigrants were devoted Catholics, many Protestants feared that they were shock troops of Roman Catholic reactionism.

_____   _____   12. Because there were more ministers than there were pulpits, and because evangelicals felt responsible for wrongs committed by Americans around the world, much money was raised to send young volunteer missionaries around the world.

VII. Important by Consequences or as a Symbol

Determine whether you believe each of the following statements to be important because of their consequences or direct impact at the time (IC) or important as symbols of those times (IS). Then indicate whether you consider the statement to be verifiable (V) or unverifiable (U). Write your choices in the blanks to the left of each statement.

IC–IS   V–U

_____ ____ 1. Thomas Gallauder was disgusted to learn that the methods of teaching the deaf to read lips and to communicate by sign language were closely guarded trade secrets.

_____ ____ 2. It was not uncommon for guards to charge fashionable people admission to asylums and goad the inmates into performing antics for the visitors' amusement.

_____ ____ 3. Connecticut used an abandoned mine shaft as its state penitentiary.

_____ ____ 4. Wine and brandy were fixtures of middle-class and upper-class life.

_____ ____ 5. Drunkenness was universally regarded as sinful and socially unacceptable.

_____ ____ 6. The phrase "on the wagon" came into being because those who stopped drinking would indicate so by climbing aboard a water wagon.

_____ ____ 7. In 1838 the Fifteen Gallon Law in Massachusetts forbid the sale of whiskey or rum in quantities smaller than 15 gallons.

_____ ____ 8. Americans were taught that the Church of Rome was the Bible's Whore of Babylon, not merely another Christian denomination but a fount of evil.

_____ ____ 9. Protestant workingmen regarded Irish workers as a threat to their jobs and to their standard of living.

_____ ____ 10. Because young men struck off on their own, New England was left with a surplus of women to take part in reform movements.

_____ ____ 11. Stanton and Mott and been abolitionists before they became feminists, and they agreed to set aside their reforms until the slaves were freed.

_____ ____ 12. Most feminist reformers were a part of other reform movements and realized that the emancipation of women depended on more than gaining the right to vote.

ANSWERS

I. True–False
1. True
2. False
3. True
4. False
5. True
6. False
7. True
8. True
9. True
10. True

II. Multiple Choice
1. c
2. d
3. a
4. c
5. a
6. c
7. d

III. Quantification
VI 1. 16
LI 2. 15,000
LI 3. 5,000; 1
VI 4. 14
VI 5. 8,400; 370,000
VI 6. 75
LI 7. 3
LI 8. 68; 32

VI. Fact–Judgment–Importance
1.	J	VI
2.	J	VI
3.	J	VI
4.	F	VI
5.	F	LI
6.	J	VI
7.	F	LI
8.	J	LI
9.	F	VI
10.	F	VI
11.	J	LI
12.	J	VI

VII. Important by Consequences or as a Symbol
1.	IS	U
2.	IS	V
3.	IS	V
4.	IC	U
5.	IC	U
6.	IS	V
7.	IC	V
8.	IS	U
9.	IC	U
10.	IC	U
11.	IC	V
12.	IC	U

⊱19⊰

A Different Country

The Evolution
of the South

"Jealous of their own liberties, and just to those of others."
"Zealous for their own liberties, but trampling on those of others."

"History can be well written only in a free country."

Voltaire

I. True–False
If the statement is false, change any words necessary to make it true.

_____ 1. White southerners sincerely believed that blacks were innately inferior to whites.

_____ 2. The Mississippi Colonization Society, founded in 1829, encouraged planters to free their slaves so they could be shipped to Africa.

_____ 3. In 1839, David Walker, a free black, stated in a pamphlet that unless whites abolished slavery, blacks had a moral duty to rise up in violent rebellion.

_____ 4. The fear of a bloody slave rebellion in the South was mostly an abstract speculation.

_____ 5. Runaway slaves in Georgia joined with Seminole Indians to raid outlying plantations and free slaves there.

_____ 6. Frederick Douglass refused to buy his freedom from his master even though he had the money and his master was willing.

_____ 7. County governments in the South were required to fund and maintain slave patrols.

_____ 8. Fitzhugh related the slaves' happiness to the spiritual conditions of their life.

_____ 9. Southern leaders were far better educated than the northern elite.

_____ 10. Most southern states upheld the right of abolitionist literature to circulate in the South as long as it did not support violence.

II. Multiple Choice

_____ 1. Slavery was still legal in New York as late as

   a. 1827
   b. 1852
   c. 1803
   d. 1861

_____ 2. All except which of the following supported the American Colonization society?

   a. Madison
   b. Monroe
   c. Clay
   d. Calhoun

_____ 3. Garrison, the uncompromising abolitionist, was stoned in Boston, dragged through the streets, and finally rescued by

   a. city police
   b. free blacks
   c. a group of abolitionist women
   d. some southern sympathizers

_____ 4. The leader of the largest and most influential rebellion of slaves in 1831 was

   a. Marcus Garvey
   b. Nat Turner
   c. Denmark Vesey
   d. Frederick Douglass

_____ 5. The South's reaction to protect their peculiar institution involved

   a. insulating the South from outside ideas
   b. ceasing to apologize for slavery
   c. reforming the state slave codes
   d. all of the above

_____ 6. George Fitzhugh argued that the North suffered from free labor because

   a. the lower classes were irreligious
   b. the lower classes were tempted by dangerous doctrines
   c. the section teemed with disruptive reformers
   d. all of the above

_____ 7. Nat Turner's rebellion of 1831 was triggered by

   a. increased brutality of slave-owners in Virginia
   b. a sudden chance to gain freedom
   c. a solar eclipse that he took as a sign from God
   d. abolitionist literature

III. Quantification

Fill in each blank in the following statements with the correct number or numbers. Then determine whether you consider the statement to be very important (VI) or less important (LI). Write your choice in the blank to the left of each statement.

VI–LI

_____ 1. In 1832 the Virginia legislature rejected a proposal to free slaves by a vote of _____ to _____ .

_____ 2. Nat Turner led a slave rebellion in 1831 that killed _____ whites and resulted in the hanging of _____ of his followers.

_____ 3. In large parts of Louisiana, Mississippi, and South Carolina, blacks outnumbered whites by _____ to _____ .

_____ 4. Turner's uprising followed the belligerent first issue of *The Liberator* by only _____ months.

_____ 5. There were about _____ free blacks in the South in 1860, _____ to every _____ slaves.

IV. Concept–Ideas

Identify each of the following key words briefly and explain the relationship between them and the words that follow in parentheses. Then rank the concepts from 1 to 8 indicating the three most important concepts in understanding the chapter.

1–8

_____ 1. freedom (future open — wills — antislavery — economics — race — inferior — division — burden)

_____

_____

_____ 2. colonization (alternative — West Africa — legislatures — Liberia — model — servitude — unknown land — cotton boom — "down the river")

_____

_____

_____ 3. phase out (Virginia — compensation — defensive — half — sad —rejection — lead — Deep South)

_____

_____

_____ 4. Abolition (morality — Quakers — souls — no moderation — no compromise — savage — mob — monster)

_____

_____

_____ 5. rebellion (personal liberty — farm tools conspiracy — runaway — imagination — fear — eight months)

_____

_____ 6. dissent (federal mails — kidnap — gag rule — bitterness — newspaper)

_____

_____ 7. positive good (defense — Bible — cultured upper class — better life — cared for — northern worker — merry)

_____

_____ 8. control (free — read — policing — two miles — religion — coded language)

_____

_____

V. Essay Questions

Write notes under each of the following questions that would help you answer similar essay questions on an exam.

1. Prior to about 1830 what were southern attitudes toward slavery?

_____

_____

2. Explain the reasons for the southerners' fear of abolitionism.

_____

_____

3. Why did colonization fail? Was this, in your opinion, ever a viable option? Why? Was it morally a beneficial approach to the problem of slavery and the existence of two races side by side?

_____

_____

_____

4. Why could one argue that a great deal of history depended on the decision of the Virginia legislature in late January, 1832? How might a reversal of the vote have changed the course of history? Be as specific as possible.

_____

_____

_____

5. What was the approach of William Lloyd Garrison to the slavery problem? Do you agree with Garrison, or would you consider him a radical who irresponsibly inflamed an issue? Explain.

_____

_____

_____

6. Describe the Nat Turner rebellion and its impact on the South. Why do you think there were not more rebellions if in large parts of several states whites were outnumbered 20 to 1 by blacks?

_____

_____

_____

7. How did the South suppress the issue of slavery? What action did southerners take that seems unconstitutional? Explain.

_____

_____

_____

8. List and explain briefly the arguments for the good of slavery offered by Thomas Roderick Drew and George Fitzhugh. In your opinion were any of the arguments valid? Explain. Attempt a reply to the arguments.

_____

_____

_____

9. What techniques were used to manage and control slaves? How might techniques like this have an impact on the white man and his society?

_____

_____

_____

10. Describe John Brown's efforts at Harper's Ferry. Would you have praised Brown or condemned him? Why?

_____

_____

_____

VI. Fact–Judgment–Importance

Determine whether you consider each of the following statements to be a fact (F) or a judgment (J). A judgment may be true and you may agree with it, but it remains a judgment because it is *derived from* fact and not a fact itself. It could be either a reasoned judgment or a professional interpretation. Determine whether you consider each of the following statements to be very important (VI) or less important (LI). Write your choices in the blanks to the left of the statement.

F–J   VI–LI

_____ _____ 1. The chief reason that southerners did not do away with slavery was the privileged position of the great planters.

_____ _____ 2. Prior to the 1830s northerners as well as southerners found nothing grossly offensive in the idea of human bondage.

_____ _____ 3. Southerners believed that race was a fundamental division of humanity and the two peoples of the South could not live side by side as equals.

_____ _____ 4. A switch of only eight votes on the bill to free slaves in Virginia in 1832 would have changed the course of history.

_____ _____ 5. Many eighteenth-century Quakers, such as John Wollman, had spoken publicly of the sinfulness of slavery.

_____ _____ 6. In 1829 the language used to express the issues of slavery began to change, and David Walker spoke in terms of violent revolution.

_____ _____ 7. Garrison and other extremists were hated in the South, not so much because they were against slavery, but because they seemed to incite bloody slave rebellions.

_____ _____ 8. Runaway slaves in Georgia joined with Seminole Indians to raid outlying plantations and free the slaves.

_____ _____ 9. The resolution to reward the capture of Garrison meant that Georgia's legislature was sanctioning a felony.

_____ _____ 10. Slavery had served as a foundation of high culture since the beginning of recorded time.

_____ _____ 11. Although the public school systems of the South were vastly inferior to those of the North, the leaders of the South were far better educated than the northern elite.

_____ _____ 12. The slave was much better cared for than the northern wage-worker.

_____ _____ 13. "A merrier being does not exist on the face of the globe than the Negro slave of the United States."

_____ _____ 14. Slave patrols, mounted posses of armed whites, policed the roads and plantations, particularly at night.

_____ _____ 15. Although black preachers were instructed to steer clear of the justice of the slavery issue, many developed coded language to convey their protest.

VII. Cause–Data–Result

Determine whether each of the following statements reveals a cause of an event (C), is merely data about the event (D), or indicates a result of an event (R). Indicate your choice in the blank to the left of each statement. Of course, many choices are a matter of delicate judgment.

C–D–R

_____ 1. Whites believed that if blacks were free, the antipathy between the races would result in chronic racial war.

_____ 2. Most blacks felt no attraction for Africa and thus only about 11,000 settled in Liberia.

_____ 3. The American Colonization Society was founded in 1817 to provide slaveowners an alternative to living alongside free blacks.

_____ 4. When the Mississippi Colonization Society was founded in 1829 the explicit purpose was to rid the state of free blacks.

_____ 5. The speeches in the Virginia legislature regarding freedom for slaves typically opened with the expressed wish that blacks had never been introduced into Virginia.

_____ 6. To Garrison, there was no more compromising with an evil institution than there was discussing sin with Satan.

_____ 7. Nat Turner drew his own interpretation of the Bible and was perhaps mystically inspired, and his rebellion was triggered by a solar eclipse.

_____ 8. Nat Turner and his followers were hanged, and other blacks, many of whom were innocent, were quietly murdered by frightened whites in retaliation.

_____ 9. Because of the emotion surrounding the issue of slavery, southern congressmen wanted every petition dealing with slavery to be tabled without discussion.

_____ 10. The Bible and the great civilizations of antiquity were used to support the institution of slavery.

_____ 11. Calhoun believed that the statement "all men are created equal," if taken literally, was not true.

_____ 12. The reason for tending carefully to the slaves' needs was practical—if healthy, they worked more efficiently and did not rebel.

_____ 13. By 1840, the states of the Deep South had adopted laws that made it virtually impossible for a slaveowner to free his slaves.

_____ 14. Religion was an effective means of control, and careful masters paid close attention to the kind of preaching their slaves heard.

_____ 15. Garrison was perhaps the least effective of the abolitionists because he alienated more people with his intemperate language than he converted.

ANSWERS

I. True–False
1. True
2. False
3. True
4. False
5. True
6. False
7. True
8. False
9. True
10. False

II. Multiple Choice
1. a
2. d
3. c
4. b
5. d
6. d
7. c

III. Quantification
VI 1. 73; 58
VI 2. 60; 40
LI 3. 20; 1
VI 4. 8
LI 5. 250,000; 1; 15

VI. Fact–Judgment–Importance
1.	J	VI
2.	J	VI
3.	J	VI
4.	J	VI
5.	F	LI
6.	J	VI
7.	J	LI
8.	F	LI
9.	F	VI
10.	J	LI
11.	J	LI
12.	J	LI
13.	J	LI
14.	F	VI
15.	F	VI

VII. Cause–Data–Result
1. C
2. R
3. C
4. C
5. D
6. C
7. C
8. R
9. R
10. D
11. D
12. C
13. R
14. D
15. R

⊷20⊷

The Peculiar Institution

Slavery
as It Was Perceived
and as It Was

"So you are the lady whose book started this great war."

"That horrid tale of perfidy and strife
Murder and spoil, which men call history."

William Cullen Bryant

I. True–False
If the statement is false, change any words necessary to make it true.

_____ 1. In Stephan Foster's songs slaves were represented as uncomplicated, loving creatures who enjoyed a secure, satisfying life.

_____ 2. It made no difference to thoughtful abolitionists that proslavery people could describe hundreds of kind and generous masters.

_____ 3. There was no documentary basis for *Uncle Tom's Cabin*.

_____ 4. The vast majority of slaves were field hands who raised a cash crop by means of heavy labor year round.

_____ 5. After 1808 it was a violation of federal law to import slaves from anywhere except the West Indies.

_____ 6. In slavery the only incentive to work hard for the master was a positive one of a reward or complement.

_____ 7. The stories of Uncle Remus make the point that wit is better than violence in dealing with whites.

_____ 8. Slaves would not dare run away unless they were convinced that they had a good chance of reaching the North.

_____ 9. Slaves were permitted to buy and sell outside the plantation but one-half the money had to go to the master.

_____ 10. One slave actually commanded free whites who worked on a flatboat hauling lumber to New Orleans.

II. Multiple Choice

_____ 1. The ingredients of Foster's South were

    a. grand houses
    b. Spanish moss
    c. the scent of magnolia blossoms
    d. all of the above

_____ 2. In _Uncle Tom's Cabin_ the good master is forced to

    a. beat Tom
    b. sell Tom
    c. free Tom
    d. return Tom to slavery

_____ 3. The popular vision of slavery came full circle—from Uncle Tom through Scarlet O'Hara and Mammy to

    a. Simon Legree
    b. Martin Luther King, Jr.
    c. Harlem
    d. Kunta Kinte

_____ 4. When an unhealthy or dangerous task needed to be done, plantation owners would

    a. pick old or sick slaves to do it
    b. hire free black or Irish workers
    c. force troublesome slaves to work as punishment
    d. turn the job over to Indians

_____ 5. An important part of the Biblical basis for slavery is the story of

    a. Jesus and the Centurion
    b. Paul and Silas
    c. Noah and Ham
    d. Ruth and Boaz

_____ 6. For slaves the only real guarantee against death or brutal treatment at the hands of their masters was

    a. their cash value
    b. the Christian religion
    c. the enforcement of slave codes
    d. none of the above

_____ 7. By the 1850s, most slaves had warmly embraced an emotional brand of Protestant Christianity that was basically

    a. Catholic
    b. Presbyterian and Reformed
    c. Baptist and Methodist
    d. Congregational and Adventist

III. Quantification

Fill in each blank in the following statements with the correct number of numbers. Then determine whether you consider the statement to be very important (VI) or less important (LI). Write your choice in the blank to the left of each statement.

VI–LI

_____ 1. The novel *Uncle Tom's Cabin* sold _____ copies.

_____ 2. Only _____ white family in _____ owned slaves, and only a minority of white southerners had a material stake in slavery.

_____ 3. In 1860 only _____ planters, less than _____ percent of the southern population, owned 100 or more slaves.

_____ 4. During the 1850s an average annual crop of _____ million bales brought more than _____ million into the American economy from abroad.

_____ 5. The cost of a first-rate field hand, a healthy man in the prime of life, was $ _____ .

_____ 6. By the 1850s a slave produced from $ _____ to $ _____ in value each year and cost $ _____ to $ _____ to feed, clothe, and shelter.

_____ 7. An estimated _____ Africans and Cubans were smuggled into the United States between 1808 and 1861.

_____ 8. By 1850 as many as _____ blacks had escaped to free states.

IV. Concepts–Ideas

Identify each of the following key words briefly and explain the relationship between them and the words that follow in parentheses.

1. old South (contented slaves — gracious people — nostalgia — *Gone With the Wind* —kindly master— sentimental)

_____

_____

2. moral belief (brutal — calous — generous — sin — novel — evil institution — subtle — documentary basis)

_____

_____

3. rhythms of labor (profit — supervise — overseer — task — gang — blacksnake)

_____

_____

4. slave economy (Mason-Dixon — material stake — few — side by side — legends — maximum labor— cotton crop — year round — unhealthy — expensive)

_____

_____

5. civil rights (none — property — buy or sell — contracts — marry — testify — travel — congregate — read)

_____

_____

6. decency (benevolent patriarch — rations — gardens — coops — work outside — sell in town — purchase freedom — whipping)

_____

_____

7. protest (irresponsible — lazy — own garden — threat — theft — no wrong — nap time)

_____

_____

8. escape (borders — visit — failure — conceal — solidarity — quality — wit — Brier Possum)

_____

_____

9. aristocracy (elegant — waited on — belle — dances — diary — finishing school — concubines — sit and talk)

_____

_____

10. slave trade (chattel property — ugly — profitable — "down the river" — coffles — disgust — teeth — handkerchief — breeders — buccaneers)

_____

_____

Which concept above do you consider to be the greatest indictment of the slave system? Why?

_____

_____

_____

V. Essay Questions

Write notes under each of the following questions that would help you answer similar essay questions on an exam.

1. Compare and contrast the Foster-Mitchell view of the old South with the abolitionist-Stowe view. Which do you believe was closer to the truth? Why? Considering these two views, what problems would the historian have in trying to describe the *real* old South?

_____

_____

_____

2. What were the important points made in *Uncle Tom's Cabin*? Did Stowe accurately understand and present the basic moral question regarding slavery? Why or why not?

_____

_____

_____

3. Describe life on a plantation. Include statistical data in your description as well as the rhythms of labor.

_____

_____

_____

4. What was involved in the buying and selling of slaves? To what extent might this be considered the worst part of the institution of slavery?

_____

_____

_____

5. Describe life under slavery. What are the most distasteful features and what are the most positive aspects? Does the treatment of the slave really matter if one person owns another? Explain.

_____

_____

_____

6. What was the Biblical basis for slavery? How would you respond to the southern argument from the Bible? Explain.

_____

_____

_____

7. List the ways slaves might protest their enslavement without violence and often without retaliation. To what extent, do you guess, can this form of protest be documented?

_____

_____

_____

8. How would runaways and church services illustrate the defiance and solidarity of blacks?

_____

_____

_____

9. What was the message and meaning of the Uncle Remus stories? Would it likely be an effective message under the circumstances? Why?

_____

_____

_____

10. Which two pictures in the two chapters dealing with the south and slavery most impress you? Explain why for each.

_____

_____

_____

11. Describe Mary Boykin Chestnut's thoughts about slavery. Give your reaction to her views.

_____

_____

_____

VI. Cause–Data–Result

Determine whether each of the following statements reveals a cause of an event (C), is merely data about the event (D), or indicates a result of an event (R). Indicate your choice in the blank to the left of each statement. Of course, many choices are a matter of delicate judgment.

C–D–R

_____ 1. The traditional view of the old South culminated in Mitchell's *Gone With the Wind*.

_____ 2. Because the minstrel show was "set" in the South, Foster turned to sentimental depictions of plantation life for his songs.

_____ 3. The hatred of slavery by the abolitionists was based not on how it worked in practice but on the moral belief that it was a sin.

_____ 4. In response to accusations of "fiction," in 1853 Stowe wrote a key to her novel that provided it with a documentary basis, much of it from southern newspapers.

_____ 5. With the ascendancy of the romantic vision of slavery in the late nineteenth century, most white Americans forgot the darker side of the issue.

_____ 6. Cotton was the most important southern product and the most important American product.

_____ 7. Since southern farmers and planters strived to be self-sufficient, there was plenty of work to be done on farms or plantations year round.

_____ 8. Because slaves rarely worked more than they were forced to, the owner of 20 slaves or less had to supervise them—bribing, cajoling, threatening, or whipping them.

_____ 9. In the late 1850s, the price of slaves soared, bringing about a demand for reopening the African slave trade.

_____ 10. Many slaveowners were moved by personal decency and by their determination to live up to the ideal of the benevolent patrician.

_____ 11. Southerners maintained that blacks were the descendants of Ham (in the Biblical account of Noah) and were doomed by God to be "hewers of wood and drawers of water."

_____ 12. Free blacks generally worked quite hard, and slaves toiled in their own gardens from dawn to dusk on Sundays and by moonlight during the week.

_____ 13. The most direct testimony of slave discontent was the high incidence of runaways.

_____ 14. Black religious services were replete with animated sermons by charismatic preachers and rhythmic singing.

_____ 15. The slaves, unable to taunt their masters in a blunt manner, satisfied themselves with quiet trickery and coded tales about their relations with whites.

VII. Fact–Judgment–Relevance

Determine whether you consider each of the following statements to be a fact (F) or a judgment (J). A judgment may be true and you may agree with it, but it remains a judgment because it is _derived from_ fact and not a fact itself. It could be either a reasoned judgment or a professional interpretation. Then decide whether each statement is very relevant (VR) or less relevant (LR) in understanding the issue of slavery. Write your choices in the blanks to the left of each statement.

F–J   VR–LR

____ _____ 1. In the industrial age of the relentless machines, it was not difficult to dream nostalgically of a South that had never been.

____ _____ 2. Abolitionists had very little firsthand knowledge of what life was like in the slave states.

____ _____ 3. Slaves were uncomplicated, loving creatures who enjoyed a secure, satisfying life under a kindly master.

____ _____ 4. The underlying theme of _Uncle Tom's Cabin_ is that no matter how well-intentioned the slaveowner, he does wrong by being a slaveowner.

____ _____ 5. More typical of slaveowners was the master who worked side by side with the slave family he owned.

____ _____ 6. Very few slaves knew what life was like on the large plantations that provided the setting for the legends about slave life.

____ _____ 7. Frederick Douglass wryly remarked that "everybody in the South wants the privilege of whipping someone else."

____ _____ 8. Slaves were defined in law as chattel, a moveable item of personal property, the same as were cattle, hogs, cotton gins, and pieces of furniture.

____ _____ 9. Slaves could not own property, make contracts, buy or sell goods, marry legally, or testify in courts.

____ _____ 10. Slaveowners and overseers did fly into uncontrolled rages and kill slaves, but they were seldom punished for their crimes.

____ _____ 11. A thinly masked form of protest was the folk tales for which black storytellers became famous.

ANSWERS

I. True–False
1. True
2. True
3. False
4. True
5. False
6. True
7. True
8. False
9. False
10. True

II. Multiple Choice
1. d
2. b
3. d
4. b
5. c
6. a
7. c

III. Quantification
VI	1.	300,000
VI	2.	1; 4
VI	3.	2,200; 1
VI	4.	4; 190
LI	5.	1,800
VI	6.	80; 120; 30; 50
LI	7.	50,000
VI	8.	100,000

VI. Cause–Data–Result
1. R
2. C
3. C
4. D
5. C
6. D
7. R
8. C
9. R
10. D
11. R
12. D
13. R
14. D
15. R

VII. Fact–Judgment–Relevance
1.	J	LR
2.	J	VR
3.	J	LR
4.	J	VR
5.	J	VR
6.	J	LR
7.	J	LR
8.	F	VR
9.	F	VR
10.	J	VR
11.	J	VR

⟞21⟝

From Sea to Shining Sea

American Expansion, 1820–1848

"Energetic gringos"

"darkhorse candidate"

"californios"

"I have written too much history to have faith in it, and if anyone doubts me, I am inclined to agree with him."

Henry Adams

I. **True–False**
If the statement is false, change any words necessary to make it true.

_____ 1. After Lewis and Clark returned from their explorations, there was increased interest in western expansion.

_____ 2. Indians charged "tolls" to traders crossing their territory to Sante Fe.

_____ 3. Stephen Austin promised that his people would obey Mexican law but retain their English language and Protestant religion.

_____ 4. The American rebels in San Antonio claimed they were fighting for their rights as Mexican citizens.

_____ 5. Santa Anna agreed to a southern boundary of Texas at the Rio Neuces, the traditional boundary of the state of Texas.

_____ 6. Andrew Jackson, a nationalist, accepted the envoy from the Republic of Texas and pressured Congress to annex Texas as soon as possible.

_____ 7. The British might have made more than a commercial connection with Texas had it not been for the legalization of slavery in Texas.

_____ 8. The Russians had established forts on the west coast, one less than a hundred miles from San Francisco Bay.

_____ 9. The Indians were not a serious threat to the large, well-organized wagon trains as long as the whites continued on to the Pacific.

_____ 10. The annexation of Texas was passed by the required two-thirds vote in the Senate.

II. Multiple Choice

_____ 1. The road to the West presented all the following obstacles except

    a. the Rocky Mountains
    b. the Spanish challenge
    c. the arid plains
    d. Indians

_____ 2. The oldest seat of government in what is now the United States is

    a. Santa Fe
    b. Jamestown
    c. St. Augustine
    d. Boston

_____ 3. Military mapmakers labeled the rolling plains west of the Mississippi

    a. Indian land
    b. Disputed Area
    c. The Great American Desert
    d. Area of Potential Statehood

_____ 4. The ten-day resistance at the Alamo

    a. showed how stubborn Americans were
    b. represented an effort by Santa Anna to preserve his army
    c. became famous in Mexico
    d. bought time for Sam Houston to raise an army

_____ 5. The American president who opposed annexation of Texas was

    a. Martin Van Buren
    b. James Polk
    c. Andrew Jackson
    d. John Quincy Adams

_____ 6. The two empires that both withdrew their claims to Oregon territory were

    a. Great Britain and the United States
    b. France and Great Britain
    c. Spain and Russia
    d. Mexico and France

_____ 7. The early attraction of Americans and British in Oregon was

    a. keeping other nations out
    b. seaports for trade
    c. rich farmlands
    d. beaver pelts

_____ 8. Death along the Oregon Trail was common particularly from

    a. Indian attacks
    b. bandits
    c. cholera
    d. the Mexican army

_____ 9. Texas is unique among the states not only because it was independent before it became a state but because

    a. it reserved the right to divide into five states
    b. it gave citizenship to Indians
    c. it was made up of immigrants from older states
    d. it was once Spanish territory

_____ 10. The deadlocked Democratic convention in 1844 finally turned to

    a. Martin Van Buren
    b. Henry Clay
    c. John Tyler
    d. James Polk

III. Quantification
Place the correct quantity in the blank or blanks in each statement.

1. While the English settlers at Jamestown were fighting off starvation, _____ poets competed for a prize in Mexico City.

2. Beginning at about central Kansas, the land rises from an elevation of 2,000 feet to _____ feet at the foot of the Rockies.

3. Stephen Austin's license with the Mexican government gave to each of 300 American families in Texas _____ acres of farmland and _____ acres of pastureland.

4. By 1834, Texas contained _____ white Americans with _____ slaves.

5. Santa Anna led an army of _____ against the _____ Texans defending the Alamo.

6. In 1843, the first great wagon train of _____ Oregon-or-Busters set out on the Oregon trail.

7. A wagon train could travel up to _____ miles a day or _____ , depending on the terrain and weather.

8. There were about _____ Americans in California in 1845 compared with _____ Mexicans.

9. Polk offered Mexico $ _____ million for California and New Mexico.

10. In April 1846, _____ American soldiers were killed in a skirmish with Mexicans in the disputed area of southern Texas.

11. The United States agreed, in the Treaty of Guadalupe Hildago, to pay Mexico $ _____ million and assumed $ _____ million in debts owed Americans for California and New Mexico Territory.

12. Polk had his eyes on Cuba, where _____ slaves might be brought into the union.

IV. Fact–Judgment
Determine whether you consider each of the following statements to be a fact (F) or a judgment (J). A judgment may be true and you may agree with it, but it remains a judgment because it is *derived from* fact and not a fact itself. It could be either a reasoned judgment or a professional interpretation. Write your choice in the blank to the left of the statement.

F–J

_____ 1. Mexico became home to the greatest of indigenous New World cultures, the fruit of the interactions between the Spanish and the Indians.

_____ 2. Jerimiah Johnson earned his nickname "Liver Eatin' " because he cut out and ate the livers of the Crow warriors whom he killed.

_____ 3. In his nationalistic heart Jackson wanted to annex Texas, but he knew it could complicate matters because Texas would be a slave state.

_____ 4. Santa Anna took the Alamo at tremendous costs to his army and executed (with the exception of a few women) all prisoners.

_____ 5. The province of Texas was prosperous, produced tax revenues, and might have been no trouble had Santa Anna not seized power.

_____ 6. Each year trappers brought their furs to arranged locations and, with buyers and Indians, traded goods and enjoyed riotous orgies.

_____ 7. The mountain men proved that, while it was a long trip, it was possible to cross overland to Oregon.

_____ 8. The Indians made a game of stealing horses from, and picking up discarded goods left by, wagon trains.

_____ 9. Politicians and newspaper editors (mostly Democrats from the South and West) began to speak of the "right" of Americans to seize lands that were being wasted under the backward Mexicans or corrupted by the decadent British.

_____ 10. Since slavery was legal in Texas, President John Tyler favored annexation in order to increase the power of proslavery forces.

_____ 11. James K. Polk was a pious man who disapproved of alcohol, dancing, and card playing but favored expansion.

_____ 12. The United States had no legal claim to New Mexico or California nor the excuse that there were already many Americans there.

_____ 13. Polk's statement that the war already existed because of the skirmish along the Rio Grande was unconstitutional because Congress alone could declare war.

_____ 14. Mexican troops at the beginning of the war were ill-equipped and led by officers who owed their commissions to their social status.

_____ 15. Many antislavery northerners supported the annexation of Yucatan Province (in what was then Mexico) since slavery was illegal there and the new state would come into the Union as a free state.

V. Judgment of Decisions

Determine whether you believe that the decision or attitude described in each of the following statements was beneficial (B) or harmful (H) in its consequences. Write your choices in the blanks to the left of each statement.

B–H

_____ 1. President Porfirio Diaz stated "Poor Mexico, so far from God, so close to the United States."

_____ 2. By the 1820s, Russian trappers had depleted the west coast of sea otters and decided to withdraw from the area.

_____ 3. Santa Anna, as a prisoner of war, signed an agreement for the independence of Texas, then repudiated it when he was freed.

_____ 4. Santa Anna welcomed the Texas uprising by Americans there because it provided an opportunity to rally the divided Mexican people around a national cause.

_____ 5. Texans considered slavery vital to their economic well-being, but in 1831 Mexico abolished it.

_____ 6. The idea of territorial expansion had a positive dignity and became a sacred duty for Americans.

_____ 7. Legal claims were less important than the mission to plant free, democratic institutions in Oregon.

_____ 8. Anti-Texan forces argued that slavery should not expand and that annexation would lead to war with Mexico.

_____ 9. Polk hinted at a war with the British and demanded most of Oregon in order to force England to settle for a division of the territory.

_____ 10. Polk was determined to go to war with Mexico over debts owed by Mexico to the United States or an incident on the border.

_____ 11. In the midst of the Mexican War, Polk, who disliked Zachary Taylor, used one of Taylor's mistakes as an excuse to divert troops to General Winfield Scott's command.

_____ 12. Abraham Lincoln risked his political career by opposing the action taken by Polk, which brought on the Mexican War.

_____ 13. The United States' decision to declare war on Mexico resulted in Mexico's losing one-third of its territory largely because the United States was strong enough to take it.

_____ 14. J. D. B. DeBow wanted the United States to absorb all of Mexico, the West Indies, Canada, and Hawaii.

VI. Ranking

Rank the following factors in bringing about the Mexican War from 1 to 8 according to your assessment of their importance. The most important would be 1, and the least important would be 8.

1–8

_____ a. Open up new territory to slavery.

_____ b. Search for military glory by generals and officers, which sometimes leads to political success.

_____ c. Belief in manifest destiny of the United States to expand and spread its institutions.

_____ d. Land hunger, desire for Pacific ports, and economic gain.

_____ e. President Polk's personal beliefs about the need to expand.

_____ f. The political popularity of expansion, favored by public opinion.

_____ g. Mexico was belligerent and quick to fight.

_____ h. The United States feared some other nations would acquire California.

1. For the two causes that you gave the highest rank, explain why you consider them the most important.

   a. _____

   _____

   _____

b. _____

_____

_____

VII. Chronology
Number the following events in their correct chronological order from 1 to 10.

1–10

_____ a. Treaty of Guadelupe Hildago

_____ b. James Polk elected President

_____ c. American army occupied Mexico City

_____ d. Stephen Austin received a license to settle in Texas

_____ e. Adams-Onis Treaty approved, settling the Mexican-American border

_____ f. First organized wagon train moved west from Missouri

_____ g. Settlement of a permanent northern boundary of the United States

_____ h. Mexico abolished slavery

_____ i. Battle of the Alamo

_____ j. Annexation of Texas

VIII. Concepts–Ideas
Identify each of the following key words briefly and explain the relationship between them and the words that follow in parentheses.

1. *Californios* (Sonoma — foot traveler — mission — simple and gracious — place names)

_____

_____

2. Great American Desert (worthless — Sante Fe trade — *gringos* — few trees — manufactures — gold — plowshare — bison — "tolls")

_____

_____

3. migration (license — law — language — Roman Catholic — numerous — tax revenues — abolish slavery — new constitution — rights)

_____

_____

4. revolution (San Antonio — six thousand — ten days — atrocity — captured independence — repudication — annexation)

_____

_____

5. wagon train (missionaries — furniture — rules — cooperation — mountain men — army outpost — wagons — mules, cattle, horses — no match — ruts — cholera — grave markers)

_____

_____

6. manifest destiny ("right" — territorial expansion — mission — democratic institutions — God and nature)

_____

_____

7. expansion in politics (annexation — two-third majority — dark horse — expansionist — waffle — liberal party — joint resolution)

_____

_____

8. promoting war (legal claim — not provoke — orders to Taylor — skirmish — debts — state of war — whigs)

_____

_____

9. victory (_californio_ allies — tactical judgment — divert troops — hero — Cortez route — occupation — treaty — payment — bitterness)

_____

_____

10. extremist expansionism (all Mexico — southerners — antislavery northerners — Cuba — grandiose — destiny — reintroduced questions)

_____

_____

IX. Essay Questions

Write notes under each of the following questions that would help you answer similar essay questions on an exam.

1. Describe the interaction and relations between Mexico and the United States prior to 1835. What specific seeds had been sown that would cause future problems? Who was at fault?

_____

_____

_____

2. Who was more at fault in the clash between Mexicans and Americans in Texas from 1821 to 1836? Give evidence and arguments for your decision. Was the clash inevitable? Explain.

_____

_____

3. Explain the important battles and decisions that led to the independence of Texas. In what ways was it similar or different from the struggle in the American Revolution? Be specific. Should the Mexicans view this as an illegal deprivation of territory? Why or why not?

_____

_____

4. Describe in some detail the Oregon area before the arrival of settlers and then the process of migration to the area. Was it a glorious and adventuresome passage as depicted in films and television?

_____

_____

5. Explain the complexities of the election of 1844, candidates, issues, events, results. Would United States history have been different had Clay stuck with his opposition to expansion and won New York? Why?

_____

_____

6. By what steps did Polk take the United States into the Mexican War? Is there any doubt that he was responsible for the war? Explain. Is this to his credit or a black mark on his administration?

_____

_____

7. Describe the major events in the Mexican War. Why did the United States win so easily?

_____

_____

8. What "dreams" of expansion appeared at the end of the Mexican War? What problems would have been created if the United States had attempted to take the West Indies and Canada? Use your imagination here and project a hypothetical situation.

_____

_____

_____

9. Write an essay about Zorro and the *californios*.

_____

_____

_____

ANSWERS

I. True–False	II. Multiple Choice	III. Quantification	IV. Fact–Judgment	V. Judgment of Decisions
1. False	1. b	1. 300	1. J	1. H
2. True	2. a	2. 7,000	2. F	2. B
3. False	3. c	3. 177; 13,000	3. J	3. H
4. True	4. d	4. 20,000; 2,000	4. F	4. H
5. False	5. a	5. 6,000; 200	5. J	5. H
6. False	6. c	6. 1,000	6. F	6. H
7. True	7. d	7. 20; none	7. J	7. H
8. True	8. c	8. 700; 6,000	8. F	8. B
9. True	9. a	9. 30	9. J	9. H
10. False	10. d	10. 16	10. J	10. H
		11. 15	11. F	11. H
		12. 350,000	12. J	12. B
			13. J	13. H
			14. F	14. H
			15. J	

VII. Chronology

a.	10
b.	6
c.	9
d.	2
e.	1
f.	5
g.	8
h.	3
i.	4
j.	7

⇥22⇤

Apples of Discord

The Poison Fruits of Victory, 1844–1854

"Henry, what are you doing in here?"
"Waldo, what are you doing out there?

"The past cannot be changed; it can only be acknowledged and learned from. It's one's destiny."

Rollo May

I. True–False
If the statement is false, change any words necessary to make it true.

_____ 1. The Wilmot Proviso, forbidding slavery in the new territories, passed in the House of Representatives.

_____ 2. Zachary Taylor, although a southerner, was opposed to slavery.

_____ 3. The California state constitution was silent on the slavery issue when California applied for admission in 1849.

_____ 4. Clay's Omnibus Bill called for an end to the slave trade in Washington, D.C.

_____ 5. Doctors tending President Taylor made him vomit, gave him a strong laxative, and administered opium.

_____ 6. The principal political goal of the new leaders in Congress in the 1850s was the gradual elimination of slavery.

_____ 7. Douglas maintained that no crops could be grown in Kansas that were suited for the slave-labor system.

_____ 8. The newly organized Republic party called for a lowering of tariffs and a strict immigration policy.

_____ 9. Jefferson Davis, secretary of war, wanted the transcontinental railroad to begin in the South.

_____ 10. In order to save the Union, Webster agreed to vote for the fugitive slave provisions of the Omnibus Bill.

II. Multiple Choice

_____ 1. Adding a clause that usually dealt with an unrelated matter to a bill under consideration is called

    a. an amendment
    b. a rider
    c. a phrase
    d. a boycott

_____ 2. The majority of gold seekers got to California by

    a. crossing the isthmus of Panama
    b. sailing around South America
    c. the Mexican route
    d. covered wagon across the west

_____ 3. Southerners believed they could not trust the goodwill of free-state senators because

    a. those senators tolerated abolitionists
    b. the southerners' belief in conspiracies
    c. of experience
    d. many of them were connected to northern capitalists

_____ 4. Who threatened to lead an army into the state of Texas unless congressmen compromised on the territory and compensation issue?

    a. Thaddeus Stevens
    b. Stephen Douglas
    c. Zachary Taylor
    d. William Seward

_____ 5. President Taylor would have vetoed the Compromise of 1850, but before he could do so

    a. the senate rejected it
    b. he died
    c. it fell apart
    d. supporters withdrew it

_____ 6. Because Stephen A. Douglas took one line with the North and another with the South he was called

    a. a "turncoat"
    b. a great compromiser
    c. a "Doughface"
    d. a "marvelous unifier"

_____ 7. The Wilmont Proviso provided that

    a. slavery would extend to California
    b. abolitionists would be arrested
    c. no one could debate slavery
    d. no slavery would be allowed in the new territories

III. Quantification

Fill in each blank in the following statements with the correct number or numbers. Then determine whether you consider the statement to be very important (VI) or less important (LI). Write your choice in the blank to the left of each statement. After some exercises there are comments on the statements. In the blank provided place an "A" if you agree that the comment logically follows, or a "D" if you disagree that it follows.

VI–LI

_____ 1. A clear _____ of the nation's congressmen did not want slavery to spread beyond those states in which it already existed.

    ___ This doesn't mean much in practice if there are two legislative houses and the sides are evenly divided in the Senate.

_____ 2. Polk did not run for reelection and died _____ months after leaving office.

_____ Since Taylor died in office after Polk and Harrison had died in office before him, the presidency in this period was too much of a strain on one man.

_____ 3. Third party candidate Van Buren took votes from Lewis Cass in 1844, thus giving New York's _____ electoral votes, and the election, to Taylor.

_____ Third party candidates should not be allowed because they thwart the will of the people.

_____ 4. California produced $ _____ million in gold in 1849.

_____ This means that it was worth the price of $10 million already paid to Mexico.

_____ 5. President Taylor owned more than _____ slaves and said that he would fight in a Civil War to keep them.

_____ This means the office of the presidency had gone downhill since the time of Washington, Jefferson, and Jackson.

_____ 6. In December 1849, Congress went through _____ ballots just to elect a Speaker.

_____ Politics had become very serious and neither section was giving in on any point.

_____ 7. The Kansas-Nebraska Act opened to slavery land where it had been outlawed for _____ years.

_____ The Kansas-Nebraska Act was a major cause of the Civil War since it raised a question that had already been settled.

IV. Essay Questions

Write notes under each of the following questions that would help you answer similar essay questions on an exam.

1. What was the argument of Henry David Thoreau in "Civil Disobedience"? Do you agree or disagree with Thoreau, Gandhi, and King? Why?

_____

_____

_____

2. Explain the theoretical debate related to the Wilmot Proviso between Calhoun and the Free-Soilers. With which do you agree? Explain.

_____

_____

_____

3. In what ways was the election of 1848 important? In what ways unimportant?

_____

_____

_____

4. Describe the California gold rush. Explain why this had political results that began a chain of events leading to extremism, violence, and absence of compromise.

_____

_____

_____

5. As a northerner interested in the moral issues of the situation, what parts of the Omnibus Bill would be disturbing? Be specific. Would you have voted for it all in order to settle the issue at the time? Why or why not?

_____

_____

_____

6. Was President Taylor's death a "footnote" to history, a trivia item, or a tragedy and turning point in the heated 1850s? Explain your judgment.

_____

_____

_____

7. Who were the new breed of politicians to arrive in Washington in the 1850s? How did they differ from the Old Guard? Was their arrival a helpful sign? Why?

_____

_____

_____

8. Explain the debate over the railroad to California and indicate how it led to the new issue of slavery in the Kansas and Nebraska territories.

_____

_____

_____

9. Was Douglas unwise in raising the issue of slavery in the territories and in his doctrine of popular sovereignty? Why? Is this a case of too much democracy or a democracy that has the potential to bring about division and violence?

_____

_____

_____

10. Why did the Kansas-Nebraska Act fail? Was it a democratic act that should have been supported? Explain.

_____

_____

_____

11. How would you have solved the problem of slavery in the territories in 1854? Be specific.

_____

_____

_____

12. Write an essay on "Life In The Diggings." Be sure to mention "poor man's diggings," hydraulic mining, prejudice, and sectionalism.

_____

_____

_____

13. Describe the encounter between the Indians and the white man between 1840 and 1860. To what extent does attitude produce behavior?

_____

_____

_____

V. Ranking

1. Examine carefully the following "turning points" (important decisions and events which speeded up developments, stopped developments, or modified and changed the course of developments) and then rank them from 1 to 12. Consider, of course, their immediate and long-range consequences. Some may be of great symbolic importance beyond the immediate reaction or results.

1–12

____ a. Douglas' Kansas-Nebraska Act

____ b. Thoreau's decision to go to jail rather than pay taxes

____ c. Discovery of gold in California

____ d. Establishment of the Republican party

____ e. Wilmot Proviso

____ f. Plans to build a railroad to California

____ g. California applies for admission as a free state

____ h. Douglas' "Compromise of 1850"

____ i. Election of 1848

____ j. Deaths of Clay, Calhoun, Webster, and Benton in the 1850s

____ k. Gadsden's purchase and the struggle over railroads

____ l. Death of Zachary Taylor

2. For the two choices you gave the highest rank, explain why you consider them the most important.

a. _____

_____

_____

b. _____

_____

_____

3. For the choice you gave the lowest rank, explain why you consider it the least important.

_____

_____

_____

VI. Chronology

1. Number the following events in their correct chronological order from 1 to 12.

1–12

_____ a. Douglas' Kansas-Nebraska Act

_____ b. Thoreau's decision to go to jail rather than pay taxes

_____ c. Discovery of gold in California

_____ d. Establishment of the Republican party

_____ e. Wilmot Proviso

_____ f. California applies for admission as a free state

_____ g. Douglas' "Compromise of 1859"

_____ h. The deaths of Clay, Calhoun, Webster, and Benton in the 1850s

_____ i. Gadsden's purchase and the struggle over railroads

_____ j. Death of Zachary Taylor

2. Give one example from the sequence of events why a knowledge of chronology (which event happened in relation to others) is important in understanding the period.

_____

_____

_____

VII. Fact–Judgment–Importance

Determine whether you consider each of the following statements to be a fact (F) or a judgment (J). A judgment may be true and you may agree with it, but it remains a judgment because it is *derived from* fact and not a fact itself. It could be either a reasoned judgment or a professional interpretation. Then determine whether you consider each of the following statements to be very important (VI) or less important (LI). Write your choices in the blanks to the left of the statement.

F–J   VI–LI

_____   _____   1. The Mexican War was foisted on Mexico and the United States by southern slave-owners who wanted to expand slavery.

_____   _____   2. The Wilmot Proviso would have forbidden slavery in the new territories taken from Mexico.

_____   _____   3. The Constitution forbade Congress to discriminate against the citizens of any state, but if slavery was legal in one state, the "property" could be moved into the territories.

_____   _____   4. Small family farmers were the backbone of the nation, so slavery had to be kept out in order for them to prosper.

_____   _____   5. As late as 1857, an Oregon law forbade both slaves and free blacks to enter the territory.

_____   _____   6. Zachary Taylor never cast a vote in his life. He refused to pay the postage due on the letter announcing his nomination.

_____   _____   7. California was never established as a territory before it became a state and was, in principle, a conquered land under military occupation.

_____   _____   8. Although the slave trade was abolished in Washington, D.C., there were slave auctions nearby in both Arlington and Alexandria, Viriginia.

_____   _____   9. In response to the defeat of Henry Clay's Omnibus Bill, Calhoun suggested that there be two presidents, one from the North and one from the South.

_____   _____   10. Douglas' manipulations to get a majority for each bill that comprised the "Compromise of 1850" were brilliant.

_____   _____   11. Taylor, had he lived, would not have signed the compromise bills of 1850, but the easy-going Millard Fillmore signed them all into law.

_____   _____   12. From a construction engineer's point of view, a southern route for a transcontinental railroad was by far the best.

_____   _____   13. Left to itself, Kansas would have become a state of small families who would have voted against slavery.

_____   _____   14. The Republicans not only opposed the expansion of slavery, but also supported a transcontinental railroad, a homestead act, a high protective tariff, and a liberal immigration policy.

_____   _____   15. The Chinese were mistreated in the mines because they looked strange and alien.

VIII. Cause–Data–Results

Determine whether each of the following statements is a cause of an event (C), is merely data about the event (D), or indicates a result of an event (R). Indicate your choice in the blank to the left of each statement. Some may be a combination of two in the same statement. Of course, many choices are a matter of delicate judgment.

C–D–R

_____ 1. Although the House of Representatives approved the Wilmot Proviso, the Senate defeated it every time it was voted on.

_____ 2. The discovery of gold brought thousands of gold-seekers to California and increased the population to the level of statehood.

_____ 3. When Van Buren took votes from Lewis Cass in New York, he gave the election to the slaveowning Whig, General Zachary Taylor.

_____ 4. Thoreau's insistence that it was a moral person's duty not to collaborate with an immoral government landed him in jail.

_____ 5. In 1849 California applied for admission to the Union as a free state.

_____ 6. Extremists refused to accept the Omnibus Bill, thus the spirit of compromise over slavery was dead.

_____ 7. Douglas tackled the Omnibus Bill by dividing it into component parts so that congressmen could vote separately on each.

_____ 8. Because California would upset the North–South balance in the Senate, it was not admitted immediately upon application.

_____ 9. During the 1850s "fire-eaters" from both the North and the South displaced moderates in the halls of Congress.

_____ 10. Abolitionists were not only hated in the South but were also unpopular with the majority of northerners.

_____ 11. The Gadsden Purchase opened an excellent route for the transcontinental railroad, a southern route which provoked northern railroad interests.

_____ 12. James Polk wore himself out and died less than four months after leaving the White House.

IX. Single and Multiple Causation

Examine the following events and developments and then decide whether each can best be explained (in a direct sense) by one single cause (S) or by multiple causes (M). Place your choice in the blank space to the left of each.

S–M

_____ 1. the rush to California by thousands of people from 1848 to 1850

_____ 2. the passage of Douglas' "Compromise of 1850"

_____ 3. the death of President Zachary Taylor

_____ 4. Henry David Thoreau languishing in a concord jail

_____ 5. Zachary Taylor's victory in 1848

_____ 6. the defeat of Clay's Omnibus Bill

_____ 7. the debate over building a transcontinental railroad

_____ 8. emergence of a lawless, unstable area in western Missouri

_____ 9. Republicans' decision to include a liberal immigration policy in their party program

_____ 10. Stephen Douglas' decision to present the Kansas–Nebraska bill

ANSWERS

I. True–False
1. True
2. False
3. False
4. True
5. True
6. False
7. True
8. False
9. True
10. True

II. Multiple Choice
1. b
2. d
3. a
4. c
5. b
6. c
7. d

III. Quantification
VI 1. majority
LI 2. 4
LI 3. 36
LI 4. 10
LI 5. 100
VI 6. 63
VI 7. 34

VI. Chronology
a.   9
b.   1
c.   3
d.   10
e.   2
f.   4
g.   6
h.   7
i.   8
j.   5

VII. Fact–Judgment–Importance
1.   J   VI
2.   F   VI
3.   F   VI
4.   J   LI
5.   F   LI
6.   F   LI
7.   F   LI
8.   F   LI
9.   F   LI
10. J   LI
11. J   VI
12. J   VI
13. J   LI
14. F   VI
15. J   LI

VIII. Cause–Data–Result
1.   D
2.   C
3.   R
4.   C
5.   D
6.   R
7.   R
8.   C
9.   D
10. D
11. C
12. R

IX. Single and Multiple Causation
1.   S
2.   M
3.   M
4.   S
5.   M
6.   M
7.   S
8.   M
9.   S
10. M

══23══

The Collapse
of the Old Union

The Road to Secession,
1854–1861

"As God made us separate, we can leave one another alone, and do one another much good thereby."

"Such is the unity of history that anyone who endeavors to tell a piece of it must feel that his first sentence tears a seamless web."

Maitland

I. True–False
If the statement is false, change any words necessary to make it true.

_____ 1. The Ostend Manifesto called for the United States to buy Cuba from Spain or, if Spain refused to sell, to take it by force.

_____ 2. The Supreme Court ruled that Dred Scott could sue in state courts, but he was not free.

_____ 3. From the Missouri Compromise in 1820 to the Republican program in 1856, slavery was always to be permitted in the Indian territory of Oklahoma.

_____ 4. John Brown was tried for treason, found guilty, and jailed until his death in 1860.

_____ 5. Many institutions split into northern and southern branches but not the large Protestant churches.

_____ 6. The Republicans in Chicago in 1860 rejected Seward and Chase as presidential candidates because they were too moderate and compromising on slavery.

_____ 7. Alexander H. Stephens, soon to be vice president of the Confederacy, was a strong opponent of slavery.

_____ 8. The reason given for the six states to follow South Carolina in secession was that the Republican administration threatened their domestic institutions.

_____ 9. The Confederacy would have nothing to do with the American Constitution of 1787 and decided to write a completely new one.

_____ 10. The guns of Fort Sumter were turned toward Charleston and posed a potential threat to the city.

II. Multiple Choice

_____ 1. In one family one son became a general in the Union Army and another a general in the Confederate Army. These were sons of

a. Robert E. Lee
b. Senator Crittenden of Kentucky
c. Salmon P. Chase
d. Simeon Cameron of Lancaster County

_____ 2. Jefferson Davis' strength was his

a. ability to cooperate with critics
b. self-confidence
c. willingness to delegate authority
d. regal bearing and dignity

_____ 3. The presidency was modified by the Confederate Constitution to

a. change the term from four to six years
b. allow for only two terms
c. remove his veto power
d. enlarge the cabinet

_____ 4. Crittenden's plan for a compromise was to be put into effect by

a. the courts
b. constitutional amendment
c. the president
d. a special commission

_____ 5. The person receiving the most popular votes in the election of 1860 was

a. Lincoln
b. Douglas
c. Bell and Breckinridge together
d. Breckinridge

_____ 6. Ralph Waldo Emerson said that John Brown's efforts at Harper's Ferry made

a. the entire nation proud
b. the South realize the futility of slavery
c. the gallows as holy as the Christian cross
d. the Civil War a reality

_____ 7. The politician who argued that slavery could be kept out by failing to enact a slave code was

a. Douglas
b. Lincoln
c. Crittenden
d. Seward

III. Quantification

Fill in each blank in the following statements with the correct number or numbers. Then determine whether you consider the statement to be very important (VI) or less important (LI). Write your choice in the blank to the left of each statement.

VI–LI

_____ 1. Dred Scott spent _____ years on free soil before returning to Missouri, a slave state.

_____ 2. One runaway slave was pursued and recaptured under the Fugitive Slave Act at a cost of $ _____ .

_____ 3. Although a majority of the delegates in the Democratic convention of 1860 supported Stephen A. Douglas, delegates of _____ southern states withheld their votes.

_____ 4. Abraham Lincoln won _____ percent of the popular vote in 1860.

_____ 5. Douglas won a mere _____ electoral votes in 1860 but he ran second, often a close second, in the North and the South.

_____ 6. The chief executive in the Confederate government was elected for a term of _____ years.

_____ 7. _____ states eventually left the Union and joined the Confederacy.

_____ 8. The North had _____ times the railroad mileage of the South, _____ percent of all manufacturing in the United States, and _____ "industrial establishments" to the South's _____ industrial workers.

IV. Descriptive–Analytical Statement

For each of the following statements indicate whether it is a descriptive statement (DS) or an analytical statement (AS). Write your choice in the blank to the left of each.

DS–AS

_____ 1. Pierce's son was killed in a railroad accident and his wife became a recluse in the White House.

_____ 2. Pierce was the ultimate Doughface, a northern man with southern principles.

_____ 3. James Buchanan helped write the Ostend Manifesto, which provided for the United States' acquisition of Cuba.

_____ 4. Fremont won a third of the total popular vote and might have defeated Buchanan had a Native- American party not been in the election.

_____ 5. The southerners had the advantages of internal lines, knowledge of the territory, a defensive war, and better commanders.

_____ 6. Alexander Stephens, vice president of the Confederacy, led a delegation to Hampton Roads, Virginia, to meet with Lincoln and arrange a compromise peace.

_____ 7. The Crittenden Compromise provided for a division of all territories "hereafter acquired" to open up the possibility of new expansion.

_____ 8. The irony of secession was that slaves could now escape to freedom in the North much more easily and that the South gave up influence in the territories.

_____ 9. Abolitionists such as Horace Greeley and William Lloyd Garrison urged the president to "let the wayward sister depart in peace."

_____ 10. Lincoln announced that the relief ship he was sending to Fort Sumter carried no military material, only food and medicine.

_____ 11. Lincoln had honed a sharp native intelligence on a whetstone of lifelong study and proved to be the most eloquent man to occupy the White House since Thomas Jefferson.

_____ 12. The Battle of Fort Sumter served both sides well because it enabled Lincoln to call for volunteers and gave the South four more states.

_____ 13. The Confederate Constitution contained curious contradictions. It defined the states as sovereign yet called the Confederate government "permanent," which indicated secession was not allowed.

_____ 14. Most northerners were shocked by Brown's raid and grimly applauded the government's speedy trial and execution of the old man.

_____ 15. Because few American whites believed in racial equality, it was to the interest of northern Democrats to accuse the Republicans of advocating racial integration.

V. Fact–Judgment–Opinion

Determine whether you consider each of the following statements to be a fact (F), a judgment (J), or an opinion (O). A judgment may be true and you may agree with it, but it remains a judgment because it is _derived from_ fact and not a fact itself. It could be either a reasoned judgment or a professional interpretation. Write your choice in the blank to the left of the statement.

F–J–O

_____ 1. Pierce was a rotten president because he did not foresee and try to avoid the Civil War.

_____ 2. The Union could be saved only if northern Democrats stood as buffers between slavery and the abolitionists of their own section.

_____ 3. From his home in New Hampshire, ex-president Pierce announced in 1861 that he hoped for a southern victory.

_____ 4. The Dred Scott case was ridiculous and without any legal foundation.

_____ 5. Taney concluded tht state legislatures could outlaw slavery but territory legislatures could not because they were subject to Congress and the Constitution.

_____ 6. Southerners wished Congress to pass a national slave code that would protect slavery in the territories.

_____ 7. John Brown's plan at Harper's Ferry was to seize the arsenal, take military equipment, and retreat into the Appalachians to encourage black rebellion.

_____ 8. Lincoln was not the best man for the job in 1861 because he suffered from melancholy and was too generous with enemies.

_____ 9. It seems clear from an analysis of the election of 1860 that the American people preferred some kind of settlement to the breakup of the Union.

F–J–O

_____ 10. By February of 1861 the secessionists had lost interest in preserving the Union but were caught up in the excitement of inventing a new American nation.

_____ 11. Buchanan's Secretary of War transferred tons of war material to the South in 1860 and 1861.

_____ 12. The state of South Carolina had to fire on Fort Sumter in order to save its reputation.

_____ 13. The "civilized tribes" that occupied Oklahoma were generally pro-Confederate.

_____ 14. The best general was Robert E. Lee, who had little in common with the Fire-eaters and much with the American national tradition.

_____ 15. The South had no business starting a war that, as Sherman said, they couldn't win.

VI. Concepts–Ideas

Identify each of the following key words briefly and explain the relationship between them and the words that follow in parentheses.

1. citizen (slave — free soil — not citizen — unconstitutional — discriminate — state legislature — territory)

_____

_____

2. runaway (conspiracy — marshalls — fugitive — mob — "underground railroad" — "conductors")

_____

_____

3. Freeport Doctrine (half slave — half free — popular sovereignty — slave code — ingenious — national code)

_____

_____

4. guerrilla (violent strike — insurrectionists — arsenals — Appalachians — black rebellions — shifting base — surprise)

_____

_____

5. treason (surrounded — capture — hanged — shock — applauded — silent — praise — massacre — police powers)

_____

_____

6. political disunity (protestants — lodges — convention — extremists — eight — federal slave code — out)

_____

_____

7. secession (unanimous — "domestic institutions" — no respect — war material — hand writing)

_____

_____

8. compromise (amendment — drills — enthusiasm — squashed — not expand — peace conference — guarantee — lost interest)

_____

_____

9. confederation (republics — laws — copied — contradictions — slavery — veto parts)

_____

_____

10. immediate steps (forts — security — delay — extremists — Union — relief ship — food and medicine — attack — loss of control)

_____

_____

11. choosing (four states — politics — troops — western part — brothers, in-laws — cousins)

_____

_____

12. advantage (material — manpower — railroads — industry — manufactured goods — navy)

_____

_____

13. "Bleeding Kansas" (Emigrant Aid — 2,000 — free-staters — runaways — Pottawatomie — scythe — extremists)

_____

_____

VII. Essay Questions

Write notes under each of the following questions that would help you answer similar essay questions on an exam.

1. What were the deficiencies of the two presidents who served in the crucial period leading to the Civil War? Would strong, aggressive leadership have made a difference? Why or why not?

_____

_____

_____

2. Explain the Dred Scott case and decision by the Court. Was this good law? Was it moral law? Explain.

_____

_____

_____

3. What was the Freeport Doctrine of Douglas? Why was it not acceptable to Lincoln or the South?

_____

_____

_____

4. Describe John Brown's raid at Harper's Ferry and the results of the raid. Should he be considered a hero or a misguided fanatic? What might have happened if Brown and his followers had escaped into the mountains with a large supply of weapons? Use your imagination.

_____

_____

_____

5. Describe the election of 1860. Include data on the Democrats' problems, the Republicans' choice, the third parties, the quantitative data, and the results. Would you consider this election the most important in the history of the United States? Why or why not?

_____

_____

_____

6. Explain the efforts at compromise to restore the Union. Why do you think they failed?

_____

_____

_____

7. Compare Jefferson Davis and Abraham Lincoln. Do you agree with the author that Lincoln was a better leader? Why or why not?

_____

_____

_____

8. Why did Lincoln decide to resupply Fort Sumter? Do you agree with his reasoning? What might have happened if Lincoln had ordered the troops to withdraw from the fort? Could the war have been avoided in these last few days? Why?

_____

_____

_____

9. What was the irony of secession? Why didn't southerners realize this before leaving the Union?

_____

_____

_____

10. What were the advantages and disadvantages of the two sides at the beginning of the Civil War? Be detailed and specific. Was the outcome inevitable as Sherman seemed to think? Did the South have a chance? Explain.

_____

_____

_____

11. Compare the economic disparities between the North and South in 1861. Could one predict the outcome of the war from these statistics? Why or why not?

_____

_____

_____

VIII. Ranking

1. Rank the following causes of the Civil War from 1 to 10 according to your assessment of their importance. The most important would be 1, the least important would be 10.

1–10

_____ a. economic differences (tariff, manufacturing, plantation, agrarian, railroads)

_____ b. breakdown of the political system (sectional parties, refusal to compromise, four candidates in 1860)

_____ c. Abolitionists and Fire-eaters (extremists, inflame, issues, emotion, anger)

_____ d. lack of trust (abolitionists, Republican president, interference with mails)

_____ e. slavery (Fugitive Slave Law, free soil, threat to institution, moral question, racism)

_____ f. political belief (Webster and Lincoln, sanctity of the Union, Calhoun and states' rights, sovereignty)

_____ g. lack of communication (not listen, not want Union, false images of each other, _Uncle Tom's Cabin_)

_____ h. poor leadership (Pierce, Buchanan, Douglas, Brooks, Sumner)

_____ i. earlier developments made it inevitable (gold in California, acquisition of territory from Mexico, death of compromises, memories of Kansas)

_____ j. two cultures (antagonistic ways of life, misunderstandings, cultural dislike, jealousy)

2. For the three choices you gave the highest rank, explain why you consider them the most important.

    a. _____

        _____

        _____

    b. _____

        _____

        _____

    c. _____

        _____

        _____

3. For the choice you gave the lowest rank, explain why you consider it the least important.

    _____

    _____

    _____

ANSWERS

I. True–False	**II. Multiple Choice**	**III. Quantification**		**IV. Descriptive–Analytical Statement**	
1. True	1. b	VI	1. 4	1. DS	9. DS
2. False	2. d	VI	2. 40,000	2. AS	10. DS
3. True	3. a	VI	3. 8	3. DS	11. DS
4. False	4. b	VI	4. 40	4. AS	12. AS
5. False	5. a	VI	5. 12	5. AS	13. AS
6. False	6. c	LI	6. 6	6. DS	14. DS
7. True	7. a	VI	7. 11	7. AS	15. AS
8. True		VI	8. three; 90; 120,000; 110,000	8. AS	
9. False					
10. False					

V. Fact–Judgment–Opinion

1. O	9. J	
2. J	10. J	
3. F	11. F	
4. O	12. O	
5. J	13. F	
6. F	14. J	
7. F	15. O	
8. O		

⊰24⊱

Tidy Plans,
Ugly Realities

The Civil War
Through 1862

"Wanted—Immediately, a SUBSTITUTE. A man over 35 years old, or under 18, can get a good price by making immediate application."

"It is a reproach to historians that they have too often turned history into a mere record of the butchery of men by their fellow man."

Green

I. True–False
If the statement is false, change any words necessary to make it true.

_____ 1. European nations dispatched officers to observe the Civil War and to compile data and lessons.

_____ 2. Jomini's rules of war called for a fight to finish without considering retreat.

_____ 3. Since it took time to reload muskets, there was a great reliance on the accuracy of shooting and hours of training went into this.

_____ 4. Bounty hunters made a lucrative small business of enlisting, deserting, and looking to enlist again for cash.

_____ 5. In the beginning, Abraham Lincoln shared the illusion that the war would be short and relatively painless.

_____ 6. The blockade of the South was effective since it prevented all vessels from making successful breaks for Europe with cotton.

_____ 7. A great Confederate blunder was to blackmail England into supporting the southern cause by withholding cotton.

_____ 8. Lee never appreciated the fact that while he was defending the Old Dominion, the southern cause was being throttled in the Mississippi Valley.

_____ 9. Although the battle of the *Monitor* versus the *Merrimack* ended in a draw, the South quickly built more ironclads in its many shipyards.

_____ 10. The Emancipation Proclamation freed the slaves in the Union slave states and in areas occupied by the Union armies.

II. Multiple Choice

_____ 1. The most worrisome problem regarding attitudes toward the war in the North was

a. Vallandigham
b. civil rights during wartime
c. defeatism
d. newspaper opposition

_____ 2. The most serious diplomatic controversy of the war involved

a. southern cotton and British textile mills
b. the seizure of two British diplomats
c. the appearance of Russian warships in New York
d. British sympathy with southern aristocracy

_____ 3. Officers who walked behind the lines during battles

a. were authorized to shoot men who panicked
b. were waiting to get up their courage
c. headed reinforcements
d. got a better view of the complete battlefield

_____ 4. All the better generals after the Battle of Bull Run emphasized the need for

a. better weapons
b. more troops
c. skill retreating
d. hard training

_____ 5. France, instead of allying itself with the headstrong cotton growers, decided

a. to concentrate on European affairs
b. to look for success in Mexico
c. to seek cotton supplies in Egypt
d. to join the North, the obvious winner

_____ 6. In 1862, Lincoln said to his cabinet that the war would be lost without

a. New Orleans
b. Richmond
c. Kentucky
d. Florida

_____ 7. The main criticism of McClellan was that he

a. moved with too much caution
b. did not emphasize training
c. refused to follow Jomini's textbook
d. was a Democrat who had sympathy with the South

III. Quantification

Fill in each blank in the following statements with the correct number or numbers. Then determine whether you consider the statement to be very important (VI) or less important (LI). Write your choice in the blank to the left of each statement. Under those you consider very important write a brief explanation as to why you consider it so important (consequences, symbolic, insightful, etc.).

VI–LI

_____ 1. By the summer of 1861, the Union had _____ soldiers in uniform and the Confederacy had _____ .

_____ 2. The basic infantry unit was a brigade of between _____ and _____ men.

_____ 3. In the North a draftee could pay the government $ _____ for an exemption.

_____ 4. Both armies were plagued by a desertion rate of about _____ percent throughout the war.

_____ 5. In the beginning Winfield Scott predicted that it would take _____ years and _____ men to crush the rebellion. Lincoln shrugged him off.

_____ 6. Richmond was the seat of the confederate government, a large industrial center, and only _____ miles from Washington.

_____ 7. At one time or another, _____ people were jailed because of illegal antiwar activity.

_____ 8. In the battle of Shiloh in 1862, Southern losses numbered _____ of 40,000 troops while the Union lost _____ of 60,000 men.

_____ 9. The southern commerce raiders, *Florida*, *Alabama*, and *Shenandoah*, captured more than _____ northern merchantmen ($ _____ million in ships and cargo) in every corner of the world.

_____ 10. The Springfield repeating rifle allowed Union soldiers to fire _____ times a minute instead of once or twice with the musket.

_____ 11. By the end of the war, _____ blacks had served in the Union Army.

_____ 12. Blacks were paid about $ _____ a month, half a white soldier's wages.

_____ 13. A total of _____ men died in the Civil War.

Which three of the above do you consider the *most* important? Justify your choices below with evidence and arguments.

a. _____

_____

_____

b. _____

_____

_____

c. _____

_____

_____

IV. Concepts–Ideas

Identify each of the following key words briefly and explain the relationship between them and the words that follow in parentheses.

1. art of war (Jomini — tactics — West Point — position maneuver — high ground — important points — weak points — exploit — twelve models — rules — retreat)

_____

_____

2. an army (cavalry — artillery — infantry — reconnaissance — mobile — harass — slugged — canister — face-to-face)

_____

_____

3. battle (double lines — one thousand yards — grapeshot — march — noise — smoke — junior officers — hand-to-hand — stragglers — bayonets — not aim — woods)

_____

_____

4. troops (17–25 — draft laws — exemptions — substitutes — riot — dodgers — desertion — bonus — at stake)

_____

_____

5. army life (waiting — digging — building — marching — profiteers — supply — physicians — disease)

_____

_____

6. Bull Run (Richmond — joking — spectators — ferocity — opportunity — hysteria — disorganization)

_____

_____

7. strategy (defend Washington — Richmond — control Mississippi — foodstuffs — blockade — bottle up)

_____

_____

8. strategy (turn back — Europe to aid — cotton — aristocracy — reduce American power — cautious — blackmail — stockpiles — Egypt — wheat)

_____

_____

9. antiwar (Copperheads— habeas corpus — post office — Vallandigham — defeatism — compromise — southern independence)

_____

_____

10. naval war (commerce — raiders — *Merrimack* — prototype — New Orleans — *Trent* — end of raiders)

_____

_____

11. Antietam (Union soil — pack of cigars — vicious — one quarter — counter attack? — "the slows" — safety)

_____

_____

12. emancipation (Union — slavery — areas in rebellion — not free any — inducement — use blacks for northern opinion — "to make men free" — British neutrality — Republican critics)

_____

_____

V. Essay Questions

Write notes under each of the following questions that would help you answer similar essay questions on an exam.

1. Explain the theories and strategy of warfare as devised by Jomini. Be specific and detailed. To what extent are these rules outdated today even in conventional warfare?

_____

_____

_____

2. Describe the procedures in actual battle in the Civil War. Would these procedures put a premium on morale and discipline in the face of battle? Explain.

_____

_____

_____

3. What were the problems in obtaining troops during the war? Were the exemptions "fair"? Why were the exemptions put into effect? Does the percentage of desertions indicate a lack of commitment to a "cause"?

_____

_____

_____

4. Describe the first major battle of the war—Bull Run. What were the attitudes of leaders and troops, the turning point, the results, and the aftermath? In what way was this battle a major turning point and a precedent?

_____

_____

_____

5. Compare and contrast the northern and southern strategy in the war. Which side had the more realistic strategy? What was the most disappointing strategy failure for the South? Could a British and/or French alliance have made a difference in the outcome of the war? Why or why not?

_____

_____

_____

6. What were the diplomatic maneuvers by the North and South? What advantage did the North have? Be specific.

_____

_____

_____

7. Explain the home front difficulties of Lincoln. Do you agree with Lincoln's disregard of civil rights during wartime? Why? Could this be a dangerous precedent?

_____

_____

_____

8. Describe the western campaign in 1862. To what extent was this the key theater of war? Was it important that during this campaign the war turned from fraternizing friendliness to bitterness and blood?

_____

_____

_____

9. Evaluate George McClellan as a general. Is popularity with and devotion to troops an asset or liability in wartime? Why did the Peninsula Campaign fail? Would its success have shortened the war?

_____

_____

_____

10. What were the gains acquired by Lincoln in issuing the Emancipation Proclamation? Be specific and detailed. In what ways could it be considered hypocritical? Was Lincoln sincere or an opportunist? Explain.

_____

_____

_____

11. Describe the war at sea. Was this a significant aspect of the war or only a sideshow? Explain.

_____

_____

_____

12. Write an essay on the conduct of battle in the Civil War. Include the factors of supply, preparation, weapons, and activities before battle.

_____

_____

_____

13. Compare and contrast the South's position in the Civil War with the American Revolution. Point out similarities and differences. Why did the American patriots prevail against the British while the South lost to the North? Use your imagination and skill of historical insight to make the comparison.

_____

_____

_____

VI. Fact–Judgment–Importance

Determine whether you consider each of the following statements to be a fact (F) or a judgment (J). A judgment may be true and you may agree with it, but it remains a judgment because it is *derived from* fact and not a fact itself. It could be either a reasoned judgment or a professional interpretation. Then determine whether you consider each statement to be very important (VI) or less important (LI). Write your choices in the blanks to the left of the statement.

F–J   VI–LI

_____ _____ 1. According to Jomini, the goal of the commander was to capture important points, take the high ground, and concentrate on the enemy's weaknesses.

_____ _____ 2. A brigadier general's brigade formed in double lines, marched in step, and advanced on a front 1,000 yards long.

_____ _____ 3. Although the Civil War became the proverbial poor man's fight, as in all wars, those who fought were young men from all classes.

_____ _____ 4. Shirking duty was not typical of either army because, whatever their resentments, the soldiers felt they had something at stake in the conflict.

5. The war mostly involved waiting, digging trenches, building breastworks, marching, or traveling on crowded trains.

6. The Confederates named battles after the nearest town while the Union named battles after waterways.

7. Had McDowell's troops cracked the southern line at Bull Run (they almost died trying), the war would have been over in the upper South in 1861.

8. Thomas J. "Stonewall" Jackson was introspective, humorless, dull, and lacking in the human touch.

9. The third strategy for the North was to use its naval superiority to blockade the South and strangle its export economy.

10. Napoleon III lost interest in the South when Mexican aristocrats offered to make one of Napoleon's generals an emperor.

11. By the time England's stockpile of cotton had run out, cotton growers in Egypt and the Middle East were bringing in enough crops to satisfy the demand.

12. Charles Francis Adams moved with great skill and energy through the salons of London and kept Great Britain out of the war.

13. Even at the bitter end of the war, when the Confederacy was defeated, Jefferson Davis insisted on southern independence as a condition of peace.

14. On April 6, 1862, while camped at Shiloh, Tennessee, Grant's armies were caught in their bedrolls by 4,000 rebel troops.

15. Compared with the minor casualties at Bull Run, compared with the losses in most battles in any war, Shiloh was appalling.

VII. Ranking

Rank the following "turning points" (important decisions and events which speeded up, stopped, or modified developments or trends) from 1 to 12 according to your assessment of their importance. Consider immediate and long range consequences. Some may be of symbolic importance even though immediate results were not great. The most important would be 1, and the least important would be 12.

1–12

_____ a. Lincoln called off the Peninsula Campaign

_____ b. Battle of Antietam

_____ c. New York draft riot

_____ d. Lincoln's Emancipation Proclamation

_____ e. Battle of the *Monitor* and the *Merrimack*

_____ f. appearance of 9,000 Virginians at First Bull Run

_____ g. Napoleon III's decision to concentrate on Mexico

_____ h. seizure of two southern diplomats by the North

1–12

_____ i. Vallandigham ran for governor of Ohio from Canada

_____ j. Egyptian cotton to England

_____ k. Battle of Shiloh

_____ l. second year of two successive grain crop failures in Europe.

VIII. Chronology

Rank the following events and developments in their correct chronological order from 1 to 12.

1–12

_____ a. Lincoln called off the Peninsula Campaign

_____ b. Battle of Antietam

_____ c. New York draft riot

_____ d. Lincoln's Emancipation Proclamation

_____ e. Battle of the *Monitor* and the *Merrimack*

_____ f. appearance of 9,000 Virginians at First Bull Run

_____ g. Napoleon III's decision to concentrate on Mexico

_____ h. seizure of two southern diplomats by the North

_____ i. Vallandigham ran for governor of Ohio from Canada

_____ j. Egyptian cotton to England

_____ k. Battle of Shiloh

_____ l. second year of two successive grain crop failures in Europe

I. Cause–Data–Results

Determine whether each of the following statements is a cause of an event (C), is merely data about the event (D), or indicates a result of an event (R). Indicate your choice in the blank to the left of each statement. Some may be a combination of two in the same statement. Of course, many choices are a matter of delicate judgment.

C–D–R

_____ 1. Two or three day's supply of rations plus 40 to 60 rounds of ammunition were issued before battle.

_____ 2. At the end of 1862 Burnside attacked an impregnable southern position on high ground near Fredericksburg, Virginia, and lost 1,300 dead and 9,600 wounded.

_____ 3. The Emancipation Proclamation ensured British neutrality and helped silence radical critics.

_____ 4. Lincoln issued the Emancipation Proclamation because he decided that he could best save the Union by freeing some of the slaves.

C–D–R

_____ 5. After the battle of the *Monitor* and the *Merrimack* the South could never build another ironclad, but the North used the *Monitor* as a prototype.

_____ 6. The Union made a greater effort in the West since the Tennessee River was of far greater strategic value than Muddy Bull Run.

_____ 7. Union soldiers fell back and then broke in hysteria, fleeing from Bull Run for Washington along with panicked spectators.

_____ 8. The attitude of defeatism, the belief that the war was not worth the expense of blood and money, was worrisome to Lincoln.

_____ 9. McClellan would not exploit his edge, perhaps because he did not want to crush the South but wanted to persuade it to give in without battle.

_____ 10. Black units were assigned the dirtiest and most dangerous duties.

_____ 11. In the fighting at Antietam, Lee lost a quarter of his army and could not retreat across the Potomac, but McClellan did not pounce on him.

_____ 12. One of Lincoln's most controversial moves was his suspension of the ancient legal right of habeas corpus.

ANSWERS

I. True–False
1. True
2. False
3. False
4. True
5. True
6. False
7. True
8. True
9. False
10. False

II. Multiple Choice
1. c
2. b
3. a
4. d
5. b
6. c
7. a

III. Quantification
VI 1. 186,000; 112,000
LI 2. 2; 3,000
VI 3. 300
VI 4. 10
VI 5. 3; 300,000
VI 6. 70
VI 7. 13,000
VI 8. 11,000; 13,000
LI 9. 250; 15
LI 10. 6
VI 11. 150,000
VI 12. 7
VI 13. 620,000

VIII. Fact–Judgment–Importance
1.	F	VI
2.	F	LI
3.	J	LI
4.	J	VI
5.	J	LI
6.	F	LI
7.	J	VI
8.	J	LI
9.	F	VI
10.	F	VI
11.	F	VI
12.	J	VI
13.	F	VI
14.	F	LI
15.	J	VI

VIII. Chronology
a. 6
b. 8
c. 5
d. 11
e. 7
f. 1
g. 2
h. 12
i. 10
j. 4
k. 3
l. 9

IX. Cause–Data–Results
1. D
2. R
3. R
4. C
5. R
6. C
7. R
8. D
9. C
10. D
11. R
12. D

≈25≈

Driving Old Dixie Down

General Grant's War of Attrition, 1863–1865

"We must make old and young, rich and poor, feel the hand of war."
William T. Sherman

"The justification of all historical study must ultimately be that it enhances our self-consciousness, enables us to see ourselves in perspective, and helps us towards that greater freedom which comes from self-knowledge."

Keith Thomas

I. True–False
If the statement is false, change any words necessary to make it true.

———— 1. Hooker's defeat at Chancellorsville seemed to confirm that Richmond could not be taken.

———— 2. Vicksburg was not of strategic importance militarily or economically but was of symbolic importance.

———— 3. Grant was not as bold as Stonewall Jackson and did not have Lee's confidence with large commands.

———— 4. Both Lee and Meade decided that the hilly area around Gettysburg was an ideal place to do battle.

———— 5. The Confederates occupied the battlefield at Gettysburg from the north, the Yankees from the south.

———— 6. Lincoln approved Mead's decision not to continue the attack on Lee after Gettysburg.

———— 7. Grant inflicted twice as many casualties on Lee as his own army suffered in the Wilderness campaign.

———— 8. In July of 1864 Jubal Early's cavalry rode to within sight of the Capitol dome.

———— 9. As Booth escaped, he shouted "Vengeance is mine, sayeth the Lord."

———— 10. Lincoln was not a popular president and was assailed and vilified by both political parties.

II. Multiple Choice

———— 1. "Fighting Joe" Hooker said that what this country needed was a

　　a. good keg of beer
　　b. general who would fight
　　c. dictator
　　d. strong president

———— 2. John C. Pemberton, commander of a Confederate force in the brush and water near Vicksburg, was a

　　a. Quaker
　　b. abolitionist
　　c. heavy drinker
　　d. brilliant general

———— 3. Although Lee's advisors urged him to send troops west to save Vicksburg in the summer of 1863, Lee decided to

　　a. train his army for the defense of Richmond
　　b. invade Pennsylvania
　　c. attack Meade west of Washington, D.C.
　　d. send troops to eastern Tennessee

———— 4. The Union line on Cemetary Ridge at Gettysburg had been curled by Lee's attack into the shape of a

　　a. dagger
　　b. triangle
　　c. horseshoe
　　d. fishhook

———— 5. The officer in command of the frontal assault at Gettysburg on July 3 was

　　a. Longstreet
　　b. Pickett
　　c. Meade
　　d. Jackson

———— 6. William Tecumseh Sherman, Grant's best general, is famous for his description of the new war:

　　a. war must be brought home to the rebel
　　b. no more Mr. Nice Guy
　　c. it is good that war is so terrible or we might learn to like it
　　d. war is hell

———— 7. Joseph Reid Anderson is an unsung Confederate hero in that he

　　a. rescued over a thousand Confederate prisoners
　　b. kept the Tredregar Iron Works of Richmond operating throughout the war
　　c. saved the life of Robert E. Lee
　　d. convinced Grant to allow the Confederates to keep the horses after surrender

III. Quantification

Fill in each blank in the following statements with the correct number or numbers. Then determine whether you consider the statement to be very important (VI) or less important (LI). Write your choice in the blank to the left of each statement.

VI–LI

_____ 1. The Army of the Potomac lost _____ casualties at Chancellorsville but Lee's losses were even larger.

_____ 2. Grant captured _____ troops while fighting Pemberton outside Vicksburg.

_____ 3. After the frontal assault at Gettysburg, _____ men were dead or wounded including all _____ regimental commanders and _____ brigadier generals.

_____ 4. Of the 37,000 muskets and rifles collected from the Gettysburg battlefield, _____ had between three and ten charges in them.

_____ 5. After the surrender of Vicksburg, General Banks took _____ rebel prisoners at Port Hudson.

_____ 6. Total deaths of the war counting both sides was _____ .

_____ 7. More than one of every _____ men who were "eligible" to die in the war did lose their lives.

_____ 8. Of the fifteen presidents who preceded Lincoln, _____ came from slave states, and _____ northerners were aggressively prosouthern.

_____ 9. By the end of the war, the income tax provided about _____ percent of government revenue.

_____ 10. The government authorized the printing of _____ million in paper money, which was worth _____ cents on the dollar in 1865.

_____ 11. By the end of the war, the federal government owed its own citizens and some foreigners almost $ _____ billion, about $ _____ for every person in the country.

_____ 12. The Morril Act granted each loyal state _____ acres for each member of Congress for the establishment of agricultural colleges.

_____ 13. At least _____ blacks served in _____ regiments of the Union Army.

IV. Evaluating Decisions and Choices

For each of the following statements determine whether the decision or choice was a successful decision (SD), made with consideration of the evidence and with intended results, or an unsuccessful decision (UD), one yielding unintended results—a failure.

SD–UD

_____ 1. Lee divided his army at Chancellorsville, left his fortifications, and hit Hooker from two directions.

_____ 2. Lee decided to attack the North rather than to reinforce Vicksburg along the Mississippi.

_____ 3. Lincoln decided to keep Grant for his effort at Vicksburg, despite the disaster of Shiloh.

_____ 4. Grant crossed the Mississippi, marched below Vicksburg, recrossed the river, and abandoned his supply line.

_____ 5. On the evening of July 2, Lee decided at Gettysburg to launch a massive frontal assault.

_____ 6. Meade decided at Gettysburg that Lee would attack at his center and concentrated every available man there.

_____ 7. Meade did not launch an attack on Lee after the last day at Gettysburg despite an impassible Potomac.

_____ 8. Grant and Lincoln decided that Tennessee was so important that Grant marched his army there and brought in 23,000 troops from the East by rail.

_____ 9. Early in 1864 Lincoln promoted Grant to the rank of Lieutenant General and gave him command of all Union forces.

_____ 10. In 1864 Grant decided that the nature of the war had changed and that his objective became the total destruction of the enemy's ability to fight.

_____ 11. Sherman ordered the people of Atlanta to evacuate the city and then put it to the torch.

_____ 12. Jefferson Davis attempted to make peace in February 1865 but insisted on Confederate independence.

_____ 13. Grant permitted officers and enlisted men to keep their horses for plowing.

_____ 14. Jefferson Davis ordered Confederate General Johnston to fight on after Lee's surrender.

_____ 15. John Wilkes Booth organized a cabal to wipe out the leading officials in the Union government.

V. Fact–Judgment–Importance

Determine whether you consider each of the following statements to be a fact (F) or a judgment (J). A judgment may be true and you may agree with it, but it remains a judgment because it is _derived from_ fact and not a fact itself. It could be either a reasoned judgment or a professional interpretation. Then determine whether you consider each of the following statements to be very important (VI) or less important (LI). Write your choices in the blanks to the left of the statement.

F–J   VI–LI

____ ____ 1. Returning from a reconnaissance mission, Jackson was accidentally shot and killed by his own troops.

____ ____ 2. Lee could never replace Jackson, and his army would never be as daring and successful as it had been in 1862.

____ ____ 3. In his rumpled uniform, the short, dumpy Grant looked listless and stupid but was actually bold and confident.

____ ____ 4. Almost by accident, the forward units of the two armies met at Gettysburg (the Confederate soldiers had been looking for shoes).

____ ____ 5. It would have been better if Lee had sat tight and forced Meade to attack since the advantage rested with the defensive position.

____ ____ 6. The troops who occupied Little Round Top (Union troops) could enfilade the open fields separating the two armies.

_____ _____ 7. Gettysburg was undeniably the turning point of the war since never again could the South launch an offensive campaign.

_____ _____ 8. Grant called off the gentleman's war and turned to battle that was not chivalrous, a war on society.

_____ _____ 9. The loss of the major rail center at Atlanta, which dealt a devastating blow to Confederate morale, was due to courageous but foolish Confederate General John B. Hood.

_____ _____ 10. Lincoln was shot point-blank by John Wilkes Booth at Ford's Theater on April 14, 1865.

_____ _____ 11. Booth was one of those unbalanced characters who pop up periodically to remind us of the role of the irrational in history.

_____ _____ 12. Booth was cornered and killed in Virginia, and four others were hanged for Lincoln's murder.

_____ _____ 13. More books have been written about Lincoln than about any other person in American history.

_____ _____ 14. Lincoln directed his generals to put Republican troops on furlough on election day so they could vote for him, while he kept units favorable to McClellan on duty.

_____ _____ 15. Lincoln won the 1864 election because the people respected his dogged will, humility, and humanitarianism.

_____ _____ 16. Black soldiers were less interested in preserving the Union than in freeing slaves.

VI. Ranking

1. Examine the following consequences of the Civil War and then rank them from 1 to 20 according to your assessment of their importance. The most important would be 1, and the least important would be 20.

1–20

_____ a. The unity of the United States would never be questioned again.

_____ b. Political dominance of the South since the Revolution was destroyed.

_____ c. Northeastern industrial and financial interests dominated politics.

_____ d. The Republican party became the "Grand Old Party" and could exploit sentiments.

_____ e. Presidents were drawn from the North and the West, except for Jimmy Carter in 1976.

_____ f. New economic legislation passed that would not have gotten through had the South been represented (tariff, railroad grants, national bank).

_____ g. The South would not have approved land grants to homesteaders of 160 acres.

_____ h. The South would not have approved grants of land for agricultural colleges.

_____ i. The Thirteenth Amendment ended slavery.

_____ j. Manufacturing—weapons, uniforms, food—was stimulated.

1–20

_____ k. The reputations of Grant and several other veterans who became presidents were established.

_____ l. The war cost the lives of 600,000 and many more suffered permanent disabilities.

_____ m. The South was devastated—its property, manpower, and morale.

_____ n. The problem of the reentry of the South into the United States had to be solved.

_____ o. The problem of race adjustment and the place of the black in American society came into existence.

_____ p. Bankers who loaned money to the government were enriched.

_____ q. The war brought sorrow and suffering into over half of the homes, in both the North and the South.

_____ r. Hatred, bitterness, and an unforgiving attitude on the part of many southerners was generated.

_____ s. The power and authority of the central government over state governments was established.

_____ t. The income tax and federally printed money was introduced.

2. For the three you gave the highest rank, explain why you consider them the most important using arguments and evidence.

a. _____

_____

_____

b. _____

_____

_____

c. _____

_____

_____

VII. Essay Questions

Write notes under each of the following questions that would help you answer similar essay questions on an exam.

1. Describe the process by which Grant took Vicksburg. Does this mark a switch in warfare regarding the security of defensive positions? Explain.

_____

_____

_____

.. Why would Grant seem an unlikely candidate to head the entire Union army?

_____

_____

_____

3. Explain in some detail the Gettysburg campaign. What "ifs" can be attached to the battle and the results (if this had happened or happened differently ...)? Do you agree that it was the turning point of the war? Why or why not?

_____

_____

_____

4. What is the policy of total war? Do you think it was necessary in 1864–1865? Explain. Do you agree with the concept overall? Why?

_____

_____

_____

5. Should Grant be considered an intelligent tactician or an uncaring butcher for his 1864–1865 battles in Virginia? Why?

_____

_____

_____

6. Describe the activities of Sherman in Georgia in 1864. Should southerners be angry at Sherman for his decision to burn Atlanta and for the destruction in Georgia? Why or why not?

_____

_____

_____

7. Describe Lee's surrender at Appomattox Court House. What would have happened if Lee had, instead of formally surrendering, told his troops (and those of other Confederate armies) to disperse and continue to fight using guerrilla warfare techniques? Use your imagination.

_____

_____

_____

8. Evaluate Lincoln's contribution to the Union. Is he to be considered a great president? Why? Is his conduct before the election of 1864 a black mark on his reputation? Why or why not?

_____

_____

_____

9. What were the results of the Civil War? Include an analysis of financing the war. Was it worth the death and destruction? Why or why not?

_____

_____

_____

10. What is your judgment of William Tecumseh Sherman? Do you agree with his decision regarding the destruction through the South? Explain.

_____

_____

_____

ANSWERS

I. True–False	II. Multiple Choice	III. Quantification	IV. Evaluating Decisions and Choices
1. True	1. c	VI 1. 11,000	1. SD
2. False	2. a	LI 2. 8,000	2. UD
3. False	3. b	VI 3. 25,000; 25; 2	3. SD
4. False	4. d	LI 4. 6,000	4. SD
5. True	5. a	LI 5. 30,000	5. SD
6. False	6. d	VI 6. 620,000	6. SD
7. False	7. b	VI 7. 25	7. UD
8. True		VI 8. 8; 2	8. SD
9. False		VI 9. 20	9. SD
10. True		LI 10. 450; 67	10 SD
		VI 11. 3; 75	11. UD
		VI 12. 30,000	12. UD
		VI 13. 186,000; 16	13. SD
			14. UD
			15. UD

V. Fact–Judgment–Importance

1.	F	VI
2.	J	VI
3.	J	VI
4.	F	LI
5.	J	VI
6.	F	VI
7.	J	VI
8.	J	VI
9.	J	LI
10.	F	VI
11.	J	LI
12.	F	LI
13.	F	LI
14	F	VI
15.	J	VI
16.	J	VI

─26─

Bringing the South Back In

The Reconstruction of the Union

"I am for negro suffrage in every rebel state. If it be just, it should not be denied, if it be necessary, it should be adopted and if it be a punishment to traitors, they deserve it."

Thaddeus Stevens

"History is little more than the crimes, follies, and misfortunes of mankind."

Edward Gibbon

I. True–False
If the statement is false, change any words necessary to make it true.

_____ 1. The reconstruction policy Lincoln proposed as early as 1863 was soundly repudiated by his own party.

_____ 2. Johnson based his care for presidential supervision on the assumption that the southern states had never left the Union because it was constitutionally impossible to do so.

_____ 3. The reaction of the blacks to the news of their freedom was to stay on the plantation as free farmers renting land from the former owner.

_____ 4. Although blacks were to be controlled economically under the black codes, the civil liberties listed in the Bill of Rights were accorded them.

_____ 5. Grant enjoyed being president and seemed to thrive in the office.

_____ 6. In the 1866 election Radical Republicans controlled more than two-thirds of the seats in both houses of Congress.

_____ 7. Some Radicals attempted to establish the supremacy of the legislature over the judicial and executive branches of the government.

_____ 8. Andrew Johnson was impeached in 1868.

_____ 9. Whatever the malfeasances of Reconstruction, the blacks could not be blamed; they never controlled the government of any southern state.

_____ 10. Governor Rutherford B. Hayes was part of the Radical Republican group that believed in equality of races and in the blacks' abilities.

II. Multiple Choice

_____ 1. When the votes were counted in the 1876 election, the popular vote went to

    a. Tilden
    b. Hayes
    c. Grant
    d. uncertain count

_____ 2. When Victoria Woodhull ran for the presidency in 1872 one of the planks in her platform was

    a. free homesteads
    b. high tariffs
    c. women into medicine and law
    d. free love

_____ 3. Reconstruction in some southern states gave birth to

    a. trade
    b. paper money
    c. modern public school systems
    d. integration of races

_____ 4. Most of the articles of impeachment of Andrew Johnson dealt with the

    a. drunkenness of Johnson
    b. Tenure of Office Act
    c. disrespect of Congress
    d. Reconstruction policy

_____ 5. Among other provisions, the Fourteenth Amendment forbade the Confederate states from

    a. setting up sharecropping
    b. paying their domestic and foreign debt
    c. integrating schools
    d. enforcing black codes

_____ 6. Those blacks who failed to sign labor contracts under the black codes could be arrested and

    a. their labor sold to the highest bidder
    b. physically punished, whipped
    c. deported to the North
    d. made to work in a chain gang

_____ 7. The rumor was that when Johnson took the presidential oath he was (because of a severe cold)

    a. incoherent
    b. a dying man
    c. unable to read his notes
    d. tipsy

III. Quantification

Fill in each blank in the following statements with the correct number or numbers. Then choose the two most important statistical statements.

_____ 1. Lincoln declared that as soon as _____ percent of the voters in a Confederate state took an oath of allegiance, the state could be represented in Congress.

_____ 2. Blacks thought the government was going to give them, after freedom, _____ acres and a mule.

_____ 3. The Fortieth Congress in 1867 dissolved the southern state governments and partitioned the Confederacy into _____ military provinces.

_____ 4. All but _____ of the 11 articles of impeachment of Johnson dealt with the Tenure of Office Act.

_____ 5. The Senate voted _____ to _____ for Johnson's conviction, _____ vote short of removing him from office.

_____ 6. The first post-Reconstruction treasurer of Mississippi absconded with $ _____ .

_____ 7. Between 1860 and 1870 the value of farms in the South declined by almost _____ .

Explain the reasons for your choices for the two most important statistics.

1. _____

_____

_____

2. _____

_____

_____

IV. Concepts–Ideas

Identify each of the following key words briefly and explain the relationship between them and the words that follow in parentheses.

1. Lincoln's plan (10 percent — allegiance — refusal — powers of president — freedom — Wade — Davis — Congress — pocket veto)

_____

_____

2. statehood (never left — punish rebels — administrative — sound theory — blame — pardon — to Congress)

_____

_____

3. Radicals (traitors — Union party — racial prejudice — equality — voting)

_____

_____

4. codes (work — second-class citizenship — agriculture — domestics — towns and cities — vote — bear arms — labor contracts — not paid)

_____

_____

5. back in union (military provinces — slavery — vote — ratify — readmitted — obstructionism — legislative control of army)

_____

_____

6. impeachment (cooperate — Tenure of Office — dismissal — articles — trial — Senate — disrespect — "high crimes and misdemeanors" — single vote — parliamentary form)

_____

_____

7. legends (degradation — bullied — corrupt — unjust — demeaning — redeem — Ku Klux Klan)

_____

_____

8. revision of legend (corruption — ludicrous — social services — public schools — New York — capital — refined — senators — cultivated)

_____

_____

9. redemption (doomed — economic foundation — poor — unpropertied — Ku Klux Klan — "white supremacy" — redeemed)

_____

_____

10. uncertain election (popular vote — three in south — two returns — commission — 7–7–1 — independent — "steal" — informal agreement — investment — troops out — disinterest)

_____

_____

11. scandal (corner gold — ruin — jobs — Crédit Mobilier — deal — stipend — kickbacks — not punished — sell stamps — morale)

_____

_____

V. Essay Questions

Write notes under each of the following questions that would help you answer similar essay questions on an exam.

1. Compare and contrast the programs and attitudes toward Reconstruction of Abraham Lincoln and Andrew Johnson. Would these programs have worked?

_____

_____

_____

2. Were the Confederate states "conquered provinces" or had they never really separated from the United States? Explain.

_____

_____

_____

3. To what extent were the Radicals morally correct in these goals? What would indicate that there was little interest in the welfare of the blacks?

_____

_____

_____

4. Describe the black codes. Were they a means of transition to real freedom or an act of suppression to overcome the results of the war? Explain.

_____

_____

_____

5. In what ways was Johnson right in his response to the Radical program? How was he wrong?

_____

_____

_____

6. State and explain the Fourteenth Amendment. Would you have voted for it? Why?

_____

_____

_____

7. Describe Johnson's campaign in 1866. Do you agree with the author that the landslide was a result of Johnson's behavior? Why?

_____

_____

_____

8. Explain in detail the Radical Republican program. Do you agree or disagree with it? Why?

_____

_____

_____

9. In what ways did the Radicals attempt to change the system of American government regarding its checks and balances? Is the parliamentary system of government more effective than the system developed in the United States? Why?

_____

_____

_____

10. Describe the impeachment of Andrew Johnson. Was this a political turning point in American history? Why or why not?

_____

_____

_____

11. What is the legend of Reconstruction (popular beliefs in the American consciousness)? What were the realities of governing the postwar South? Should the legend be revised? Why or why not?

_____

_____

_____

12. Describe the election of 1876 in detail. Is this election a black mark on American society? Why? Did the North betray the blacks and the nation by their withdrawal and deal of 1876? Explain.

_____

_____

_____

13. Describe the Black Friday scandals in the Grant administration. Should Grant be held responsible? Why or why not?

_____

_____

_____

VI. Ranking

1. Rank the following events and decisions from 1 to 10 according to your assessment of their importance. The most important would be 1, and the least important would be 10.

1–10

_____ a. decision by the special commission to declare Hayes elected

_____ b. organization of the Ku Klux Klan

_____ c. death of Lincoln

_____ d. Johnson's veto of the Freedman's Bureau Bill indicating his opposition to racial equality

_____ e. withdrawal of troops from South Carolina, Florida, Louisiana

_____ f. Grant's victory in the 1868 election with the aid of black votes

_____ g. vote by the Senate not to convict Andrew Johnson

_____ h. Liberal Republicans proclaimed Radical Reconstruction a failure

_____ i. *Ex parte Milligan* decision by the Supreme Court declaring the military had no power in the areas free of hostilities

_____ j. mob action against blacks in several southern cities

2. For the two choices you gave the highest rank, explain why you consider them the most important.

a. _____

_____

_____

b. _____

_____

_____

VII. Chronology

Number the following events and decisions in their correct chronological order from 1 to 10.

1–10

_____ a. decision by the special commission to declare Hayes elected

_____ b. organization of the Ku Klux Klan

_____ c. death of Lincoln

_____ d. Johnson's veto of the Freedman's Bureau Bill indicating his opposition to racial equality

_____ e. withdrawal of troops from South Carolina, Florida, Louisiana

_____ f. Grant's victory in the 1868 election with the aid of black votes

_____ g. vote by the Senate not to convict Andrew Johnson

_____ h. Liberal Republicans proclaimed Radical Reconstruction a failure

_____ i. _Ex parte Milligan_ decision by the Supreme Court declaring the military had no power in the areas free of hostilities

_____ j. mob action against blacks in several southern cities

VIII. Fact–Judgment–Importance

Determine whether you consider each of the following statements to be a fact (F) or a judgment (J). A judgment may be true and you may agree with it, but it remains a judgment because it is _derived from_ fact and not a fact itself. It could be either a reasoned judgment or a professional interpretation. Then determine whether you consider the statement to be very important (VI) or less important (LI) to understanding Reconstruction. Write your choices in the blanks to the left of each statement.

F–J   VI–LI

_____ _____ 1. Reconstruction was a tragic mistake: well meaning and idealistic, but doomed because of the incapacity of the blacks to act as citizens.

_____ _____ 2. Abraham Lincoln comes down to us as a heroic and sainted figure only because he did not survive the Civil War.

_____ _____ 3. Johnson was unsubtle, willful, stubborn, and blind to circumstances and personalities.

_____ _____ 4. As soon as Johnson announced tht he would adopt Lincoln's plan, the rich former slave owners began to assume southern leadership.

_____ _____ 5. Johnson's interpretation of the Constitution was reasonable, but he refused to recognize political realities.

_____ _____ 6. Far from providing the 40-acre farms that blacks thought they were going to be granted, the Johnson state governments did not even establish a system of employment.

_____ _____ 7. Debts were not to be repaid by the Confederate government according to the Fourteenth Amendment.

_____ _____ 8. Although Midwesterners liked red-hot debates between politicians, they disapproved of Johnson's campaign.

_____ _____ 9. Johnson refused to obey the Tenure of Office Act and dismissed the single radical in his cabinet.

_____ _____ 10. Sharp and vulgar language does not qualify as the "high crimes and misdemeanors" that the Constitution lists as the reasons for impeachment.

_____ _____ 11. Only through heroic efforts did the whites redeem the southern states from the corrupt and unjust "Black Reconstruction" governments.

_____ _____ 12. The modern public school systems in some southern states were not founded until the Reconstruction.

_____ _____ 13. Reconstruction was doomed from the day Congress rejected proposals to provide "forty acres and a mule" for every family of freedmen.

_____ _____ 14. Carpetbaggers were interested in making money in the process of developing the South, not as mere exploiters.

_____ _____ 15. Congress outlawed and effectively suppressed the Ku Klux Klan, but in many areas blacks were no longer voting.

IX. Cause–Data–Results

Determine whether each of the following statements is a cause of an event (C), is merely data about the event (D), or indicates a result of an event (R). Indicate your choice in the blank to the left of each statement. Of course, many choices are a matter of delicate judgment.

C–D–R

_____ 1. To provide for a rapid reconciliation of the sections, Lincoln proposed his 10 percent plans.

_____ 2. Lincoln's plan made no provision for the states of the freedmen, former slaves.

_____ 3. Lincoln cancelled the Wade-Davis Congressional plan with a pocket veto.

_____ 4. Johnson proposed his program for Reconstruction on the assumption that southern states had never left the Union.

_____ 5. When blacks heard the news of their freedom, they left plantations and farms and congregated in cities or ramshackled camps.

_____ 6. Stevens, Julian, Sumner, and Wade were committed to the principle and practice of parliamentary government.

_____ 7. The Fourteenth Amendment not only applied to the South but also cancelled any state laws that forbade blacks to vote.

_____ 8. In 1868, because of the black vote, six states were readmitted into the Union.

_____ 9. After two months, the Senate voted 35 to 19 for conviction, thus Johnson remained in office by 1 vote.

_____ 10. If Johnson have been convicted, it would have been a major step toward the parliamentary form of government.

_____ 11. The Fifteenth Amendment forbade the states to deny the vote to any person on the basis of "race, color, or previous condition of servitude."

_____ 12. The Ku Klux Klan was founded in 1868 by former slave trader and Confederate general Nathan Bedford Forrest.

_____ 13. The special commission voted on strict party lines, 8 to 7, thus giving Rutherford B. Hayes the presidency by a single electoral vote.

_____ 14. Because blacks as slaves had been the backbone of the southern workforce, the southern legislatures expected blacks to bring in the crops after the war.

_____ 15. In 1866 the Congress picked up enough support to pass both the Freedmen's Bureau Bill and the Civil Rights Bill over Johnson's veto.

_____ 16. Greely could not win in 1872 because he invited ridicule with a round, pink face, close-set beady eyes, and white chin whiskers.

ANSWERS

I. True–False

1. True
2. True
3. False
4. False
5. False
6. True
7. True
8. True
9. True
10. False

II. Multiple Choice

1. a
2. d
3. c
4. b
5. b
6. a
7. d

III. Quantification

1. 10
2. 40
3. 5
4. 2
5. 35; 19; 1
6. 415,000
7. half

VII. Chronology

a. 3
b. 4
c. 9
d. 10
e. 2
f. 7
g. 6
h. 8
i. 1
j. 5

VIII. Fact–Judgment–Importance

1.	J	LI
2.	J	LI
3.	J	VI
4.	F	VI
5.	J	VI
6.	F.	VI
7.	F	LI
8.	J	LI
9.	F	VI
10.	J	VI
11.	J	LI
12.	F	VI
13.	J	VI
14.	J	LI
15.	F	VI

IX. Cause–Data–Result

1. C
2. D
3. D
4. C
5. 4
6. D
7. D
8. C
9. R
10. R
11. D
12. D
13. R
14. C
15. R
16. C